ANCHORING YOUR WELL BEING:

A GUIDE FOR CONGREGATIONAL LEADERS

*How to Enable Your Church to Become
a Whole-Person Christian Wellness Center*

Howard Clinebell, Ph.D.

UPPER ROOM BOOKS
NASHVILLE

ANCHORING YOUR WELL BEING:
A GUIDE FOR CONGREGATIONAL LEADERS

© 1997 by Howard Clinebell

The Upper Room Web site: http://www.upperroom.org

Cover Art Direction: Michele Wetherbee
Cover Design: Michele Wetherbee
Interior Design and Layout: Nancy Cole
First Printing: December 1997

Library of Congress Cataloging-in-Publication Data
Clinebell, Howard John, 1922–
    Anchoring your well being : a guide for congregational leaders /
  Howard Clinebell.
       p. cm.
    ISBN 0-8358-0822-X
    1. Christian life. 2. Church group work. I. Title.
  BV4501.2.C585   1997
  261.8'321--dc21   97-9346
                                            CIP

Printed in the United States of America

Contents

93528

Introduction

Helping Your Faith Community become a Center of Spiritually Empowered Healing and Health

Welcome to *Anchoring Your Well Being* leader's guide! It provides two things—answers to questions frequently raised concerning setting up and leading well being classes and programs in congregations and other church-related organizations, and guidelines for the eight sessions of such events. I hope this material will guide persons responsible for planning and directing the education, small group and health ministries of congregations, including clergy and lay leaders, Christian educators and teachers, and the leaders of the network of small and large groups in congregations. I am also writing for chaplains, administrators, and staff members of other religious organizations, including church-related schools, hospitals, and other health care agencies.

I hope that you will read all of the first section. I have arranged it in a question-and-answer format to answer many of the questions addressed to me in seminars, workshops, and other events. If you have a clear idea of what you want to do in the area of Christian lifestyle wellness, I suggest that you save precious time by only scanning this section to see if there are suggestions that might increase the effectiveness of what you have in mind.

PART I:

ANSWERS TO QUESTIONS OFTEN ASKED; SCHEDULES AND FORMS

1. Questions Often Asked

Q. *Why should I begin a wellness program when my schedule and my organization's schedule are overloaded?*

A. Good question. If your lifestyle is overloading you with stress, pruning your schedule is the place to start. Do this by using life-work planning on a continuing basis. You will find brief instructions for doing this in chapter 6 of the *Anchoring Your Well Being* participant's workbook and a fuller version in chapter 6 of *Well Being*. This material will guide you in prioritizing your life and career goals so as to invest more time in the things that are most important to you and less time in other matters. Encourage your church leaders to use the same process to streamline the program schedule in light of the more and less important goals of a Christian congregation.

Then, consider these reasons that support the view that such a program should have a place in any ministry that's relevant to people's urgent needs in today's violent, high-pressure, sickness-plagued society:

1. A wellness ministry is an effective response to the needs of many people for spiritual help and guidance in living healthier lifestyles. Such a program invests your leadership energies and your organization's program time in producing the spiritually energized healing and growth that Christian people and organizations seek to maximize.

2. Christians strive to follow a marvelous healer who through most of the church's history has been called the "great physician." The acute health-care crisis in our time creates unprecedented needs for religious people and their organizations to follow Jesus' teachings in new paths, responding in innovative, imaginative ways. An effective wellness program can enable persons of all ages to discover personal meaning in what the most lyrical of the gospels

calls "life in all its fullness" (John 10:10, NEB). This was Jesus' purpose in coming. Life in all its fullness is what is called "well being," "wholeness," or "wellness" in contemporary language.

3. Abundant evidence shows that spiritual and ethical issues are crucial factors in determining the degree of health or sickness that people experience. Therefore, religious organizations and clergy have indispensable roles to use their unique resources and expertise in helping heal human brokenness and nurture wellness in our society.

4. Congregations and other religious institutions are ideally equipped and positioned to become major providers of the programs of prevention-through-wellness education that our society needs to have widely available at minimal cost Why is this need for prevention so great? Only a tiny percentage of health care dollars is spent on prevention—estimated to be only 2 percent to 3 percent in the United States. Most of the high-tech, super-costly approaches that produce modern medical miracles are focused on treatment of trauma, and on acute and chronic illnesses.

These can be life-saving blessings when needed, but they leave a near vacuum in the equally vital area of prevention. Without widespread prevention programs, illnesses will continue to proliferate, accompanied by runaway treatment costs, and countless people will miss the joys of developing higher level wellness.

Religious organizations have unparalleled opportunities to help fill this yawning health care chasm. Government and secular health agencies should do far more preventive education, but churches can and should become major providers. They can do so in innovative ways that are far less expensive than those provided by government and secular agencies. More important, doing so is a life-enhancing expression of their reason for being.

Even if your congregation has been involved in healing and health ministries, it probably has only scratched the surface of the opportunities now open to religious groups.

A timely response to these opportunities is to create innovative programs of whole-person healing and preventive, health-enhancing education.

Religious institutions are challenged today to become gardens where everyone's health can be nurtured and enhanced throughout their lives. Holistic, spiritually empowered prevention of personal and family health problems is a no-lose investment in which people contribute to their own wellness by helping to develop and participating in effective wellness programs.

5. Millions of people in our society are hurting because of self-care neglect that produces high rates of stress-induced illnesses and low levels of the life-celebrating wellness that robust health undergirds. The severe health-care / sickness-care crisis in our society poses painful problems for people particularly those in the economic underclasses.[1] Many Christians know that they need to increase their health-care knowledge and practices to achieve the multiple benefits of increased fitness. They are searching for new paths to healthier Christian living. Those who sense that there is an intimate connection between

---

[1] What is the nature of this sickness-care/health-care crisis? It has many aspects, including: (a) the spiraling cost of medical treatment. In the United States the increase has been nearly twice the rate of general inflation; medical treatment costs consume almost 9 percent of the country's GNP; (b) the lack of a safety net of assured medical care for millions of people in both poor countries and affluent countries like the United States; (c) the skyrocketing cost of medical treatment for the chronic diseases of aging populations; (d) gross inadequacies of health care for the under-class, including the working poor, the homeless, migrant workers, the unemployed, and native peoples; (e) increasing depersonalization of much medical practice resulting from high-tech, biochemically oriented, growing specialization medicine; (f) lack of holistic training for many physicians who are unaware of the psychological,

(Footnote continued on next page)

health and Christian living welcome and support
wholeheartedly church programs that offer wellness tools
and resources.

Q. *What benefits have churches with
wellness programs reported?*

A. Good news! Clergy and lay leaders usually report that
such programs are among the most rewarding and
appreciated parts of congregations' overall ministries.
Several have said that, after an initial wellness group,
requests for additional offerings come from members who
have heard about the first one from enthusiastic participants. Because of rewards like the following, wellness work

---

(Footnote continued from previous page)
emotional, and spiritual causes of many illnesses; (g) widespread unnecessary surgery and clinical Iatrogenesis, meaning
illnesses caused by hospitalization and physicians. See Ivan
Illich, *Medical Nemesis: The Expropriation of Health* (N.Y.:
Pantheon Books, 1976); (h) overprescribing of drugs,
particularly to women and the elderly, resulting in increasing
prevalence of addictions; and (i) the staggering costs of treating
the AIDS pandemic.
   This sickness care/health care crisis will be resolved only if
several things occur. There must be drastic changes in medical
education and in the medical delivery system to make the
marvels of modern medicine available to all who need them.
The exaggerated, god-like misperception of physicians as
possessing magical healing powers must be changed. Instead,
people need to have respect for the healing forces in everyone
and the awareness that each person is ultimately responsible for
the self-care that is necessary for high-level wellness. Equally
important, as spelled out in this guide, churches and schools
(and other people-serving organizations and workplaces), must
respond to the crisis by developing a network of innovative
programs of whole-person prevention, including support of
those experiencing crises, griefs, and chronic illnesses and
disabilities.

tends to move up the scale of a congregation's missional priorities :

1. A priceless reward is experiencing God's liberation of persons who had been trapped in low levels of mind-body-spirit wellness. They are freed to live life in increasing fullness. In the healing, growth-nurturing context of caring, sharing well being groups, it's inspiring to experience and participate in such miracles of transformation.

2. Another reward is discovering, perhaps to your surprise, that the interpersonal and spiritual climate of a whole congregation is gradually become more healing and growth-stimulating. This occurs when even a few peoples' whole self has been enlivened to greater wholeness. As in Jesus' parable of the woman baking bread, their influence gradually leavens the life of the community of shared faith. To become aware that one's congregation is becoming a wider channel for the flow of the healing love and justice of the divine Spirit truly is wonder-full!

3. Another reward is witnessing people being motivated and equipped to reach out more effectively as channels of God's healing in the lives of other individuals and in our turbulent society caught in the chaos of accelerating pandemics of social change. These outreach dimensions take place when Christians sense that, to be true to the biblical vision of wellness, their self-care must include care of other persons as well as action to enhance the health of their community, society, and world for everyone in it.

4. Another potential reward of wellness programs is watching one's organization touch the lives of more individuals and families in greater depth. To be "people for others" as well as for their own members, a congregation's well being programs should always be open to their community. A fringe benefit of such programs is that they can be strategic pathways to attract some community participants to a congregation's wider life.

Not long ago I received a phone call from a man in a church I once pastored on Long Island in New York. He reported with obvious joy that his young adult son, who had been "turned off to the church," had been attracted to the well being program of that congregation. The son has become actively involved in that church in ways that are producing significant positive changes in his life, the father said.

5. Another benefit of wellness programs is that they are ideal ways to involve health professionals and teachers as resource persons with needed professional expertise. Such professionals, both within a congregation and from its community, often welcome invitations to serve as volunteer resource-givers or facilitators in congregational wellness programs. Their contributions and guidance can be invaluable in designing as well as co-teaching such programs.

6. A serendipitous reward of starting a well being emphasis, for overloaded clergy and lay congregational leaders, is that such a program usually offers opportunities for them to enhance their own wholeness. Church leaders who are most effective in leading such groups are those who use these opportunities to grow in wellness as others are doing the same. This is one answer to the widespread problem of clergy and church leader burnout and burnup!

Q. *What problems have churches with wellness programs reported?*

A. Any activity involving members of our human species produce at least occasional conflict and tensions, of course. Fortunately, when church health-enhancement programs are evaluated in terms of their cost-benefit ratios, the benefits almost always far outweigh the costs. Furthermore, difficulties in these programs are quite minimal and short-lived, in most cases. This is true as long as the primary focus is on education for prevention and professional services such as blood pressure screening are provided by nurses (including parish nurses) or other qualified health professionals.

As you would expect, Christians who believe that churches should limit their ministries to "spiritual" issues may be critical. But their objections can change to affirmations if they can be helped to understand why all aspects of human life have spiritual dimensions. Presenting the biblical and theological reasons why health enhancement is essential in Christian lifestyle ministries today can also allay such criticisms.

Q. *Are there guidelines for designing an effective well being program?*

A. Based on experiences in various sizes and types of congregations and other religious settings, here are some guidelines for initiating and developing a dynamic wholeness program in your organization or group:[2]

1. Scan the texts, making notes about what seems relevant to your situation. If possible, take one or more of the checkups in these books and start to create your own health-care plan. In this way, you'll begin to get the feel for intentional fitness self-care. Your energy for trying such a program with others may increase as you do so.

2. Encourage a core group of your leaders, teachers, health professionals, and people growing in recovery programs to scan the material. Ask them for feedback about the idea of giving a wellness ministry priority in your faith community's programs. Or have a lively brainstorming session of ways to respond to the health-care needs of your congregation. A tentative plan may emerge. Ownership of the plan by some in the exploratory group who created it is one strength of this approach.

There are strategic advantages in involving church school teachers in exploratory reading and discussions with you or with the exploratory group. As they generate ideas and enthusiasm sparked by their reading and discussion, they are much more likely to offer well being programs in

---

[2]These guidelines are adapted from general guidelines for secular as well as religious organizations found on pages 309–311 in *Well Being*.

their classes. Those who have satisfying experiences in a
wellness session or group will bring contagious energy and
conviction to their teaching on this topic. Furthermore,
sharing their own positive experiences with students and
also modeling constructive health principles will increase
their teaching's positive impact.

Be sure to include your organization's chief admin-
istrative committee in making the decision about whether to
include wellness programs as a regular service. If a "go"
decision is made, the next step is to make sure that a particular committee or group takes responsibility for planning
and implementing this ministry. If the present structure
already has a logical place to put this responsibility—an
education or caregiving committee, for example—this may
be just the place.

If such committees are already overloaded, then form an
ad hoc well being task group. Linking the new group with
established structures will strengthen its hand. The committee should include members of the healing and therapy
professions, as well as teachers who bring expertise that can
be useful in planning health education classes and events.
Nurses, being broadly holistic in their training, often are
outstanding members of such a task group. And those who
were enthusiastic participants in earlier brainstorming
usually welcome an invitation to join the task group.

3. The responsible well being group or committee
should do a formal or informal evaluation of the wellness
needs of your congregation's members and potential
members. It also should evaluate the overall healthfulness of
your organization. The congregational checkup at the end
of this section is designed to be used to get such evaluative
feedback. An analysis of the findings of this survey will
enable you to identify ways to increase the overall healing,
caring, and wellness impact of your organization.

4. In light of unmet wellness needs discovered in this
evaluation, decide on the major objectives that need to be
achieved. Then prioritize these objectives in terms of their

importance and their feasibility, outlining an overall well being program for your organization. The two master objectives to keep in mind while designing this program are: (1) to make lifelong wellness learning easily available and attractive to the maximum number of people in all age groups; and (2) to make your organization a more healing, wholeness-nurturing environment for all those whose lives it touches.

5. Then develop practical strategies aimed at moving toward high-priority, achievable objectives in the well being program. Be sure to spell out who will take responsibility for implementation, who else will need to be involved, timelines for focusing on each part of the program, resources that will be required, and how you will measure its effectiveness to guide re-strategizing.

6. Two parallel strategies have been found to be effective in beginning a wellness program or strengthening this emphasis where it already exists, as it does in many congregations. First, encourage the teachers or leaders of ongoing classes and groups such as those for youth, couples, men, and women, to include a study series on a theme such as "Christian Living in the Seven Dimensions of Wellness" in their curricula. Those responsible for programming in such groups often are looking for topics relevant to their members' interests and needs. This causes them to be receptive to suggestions about wellness themes.

Second, set up one or more time-limited special interest groups for persons with particular and prominent unmet wellness needs identified by respondents to the evaluation. To illustrate, congregations with a sizable number of seniors have had good responses to wellness groups on themes such as "Growing Through Life Transitions and Losses" and "Christian Resources for Staying Alive All Your Life." Some congregation have found it effective to offer special wellness series to their entire church family during special seasons of the church year—for example, a series of eight sessions during Lent.

7. In all well being events, solicit evaluative oral or written feedback regularly from both group leaders and participants. Near the end of a session, for example, ask questions such as the following and invite honest feedback: What did you find helpful in today's session? What would make future sessions more helpful? Knowing what the pluses and minuses were from the perspectives of participants can provide invaluable guidance in designing future wellness events. Receiving such feedback half way through a series can guide mid-course corrections. If a single session is only a mini-introduction to well being, the closing evaluation should identify persons who want additional sessions to explore the seven dimensions in more depth.

8. As a seed-planting operation, if you are a clergy-person, preach a sermon or a series on a topic such as "Walking the Sevenfold Path of Christian Well Being in Troubled Times." Invite church members in health professions to stand during the service to be recognized. Or perhaps invite one or two to speak briefly about how they see their work as an expression of their Christian lifestyle and mission. After the service or services, invite interested worshipers to stay for a post-sermon dialogue and debriefing session for a half-hour or so. Or offer a longer dialogue opportunity to interested people, at a later time during the week.

During such sermons or talks, be sure to share how-to suggestions. These are practical action options such as reading in one or both texts, developing their own health care plans, or getting involved in a wellness study group. From among those who respond, at least a few persons will emerge who are keenly enough motivated to have some role in helping to create a well being program designed to meet self-care needs within the congregation and community.

9. Take full advantage of the fact that both texts—*Well Being* and the *Anchoring Your Well Being* participant's workbook—are do-it-yourself tools. As people use these

resource books, on their own or in formal groups, urge them to take the checkups, try some of the experiential exercises, jot down their issues and insights, and, most important, begin to develop their tailor-made health-care plans. People will be encouraged to use the books regularly as workbooks on their own if multiple copies are placed in the church lending library and/or made easily available for purchase by those who want their own copies.[3]

10. A superb way to highlight health issues and to launch a well being program is to celebrate a Christian wellness week in your organization. A congregation in southern California begins its annual wellness week with a Sunday service highlighting the spiritual and scriptural foundations of concern for wholeness in both the worship and sermon. Special well being programs are offered during the following week. A community health fair on Saturday makes a wide variety of practical resources available to those in the congregation and in its larger community. Community health agencies are invited to have booths at the fair offering information and resources on a whole spectrum of wellness lifestyle concerns.

These include such crucial issues as AIDS, suicide prevention, family planning, child health care, domestic violence, peacemaking, environmental caring, nutrition, and other ways to enhance individual and community wellness.

11. Make sure your organization practices what it preaches in the area of wellness. For example, encourage eating-for-wellness by serving nutritious snacks, rather than the junk food loaded with refined sugar, fat, and caffeine served in many church meetings. Do the same at church meals. Provide guidelines for those who come to potlucks to

------

[3] Having multiple copies for purchase at the opening session of a series can stimulate home use of the books. If a church's Christian education or wellness task group's budget has funds available, it will encourage home use if a discount is offered.

"bring a tasty and healthy dish." Explain the reasons for this, using this opportunity to offer guidelines on practicing healthy eating as a Christian discipline of respect for our bodies.

A church's programs should also model environmental caring by earth-friendly practices. These can include recycling all paper, cardboard and metal waste, assiduously avoiding the use of non-biodegradable plastics and throw-away materials; saving energy and water; and carpooling to all church meetings.

12. Another crucial area in which to practice what we preach relates to the well being of society. Make sure that your organization's funds are invested in socially responsible companies that follow wholeness-engendering policies. These include respect for economic and social justice, gender equality, community and environmental responsibility, non-racist and non-ageist practices. Socially responsible investments do not support industries that damage health—e.g., the tobacco establishment, the arms industries, etc., nor support national or transnational corporations that support racial or gender discrimination, economic exploitation, political oppression, and ecological damage to the earth, God's wonderful creation.

In the same direction, an essential part of a Christian organization's well being program is to mobilize the public and political influence of individuals within it and the organization as a whole to support constructive health care, justice, peacemaking, and environmental legislation on all levels—local, state, regional, national, and global—in both church and governmental circles.

Network with regional, national, and international branches of your denomination as well as ecumenical and interfaith groups on issues to help heal our society's social malignancies, including economic oppression and poverty, excessive wealth in the hands of a few, environmental damaging practices, and the oppression of groups of people, including women, ethnic minorities, the disabled, immigrants, and gays. It is important to undergird these social responsibility-justice dimensions of your church's well being programs by the prophetic voices of the Hebrew scriptures and by the policy statements of most of the mainline Christian denominations.

13. A church-based well being program should take full advantage of the unique assets of congregations as multi-generational organizations. In light of the demographic distribution of your organization, make sure that the well-ness needs of all the life stages, both genders, and those in all types of family and friend constellations, are provided for in the program. Unmet healing and health needs of seniors are an escalating problem that need to be given high priority, particularly in congregations which serve many older people. Transgenerational wellness education events and parent education-for-wellness classes are of strategic impor-tance. Such events can enable parents of children and teens to learn how to model and teach high-level wellness prac-tices in their families.

14. A significant opportunity in most congregations is created by the presence in their membership of numerous professionals in the medical care and other therapeutic and teaching fields. To utilize this opportunity, a well being plan in such congregations should include innovative ways to enrich their commitment to whole-person, spiritually-centered healing and education, for the wellness benefits of their patients or clients. Regular gatherings of such persons can facilitate inter-professional dialogue and collaboration in the congregation's well being program, as well as in their day-by-day professional practice. By thus encouraging friendships and mutual understanding of other profes-sionals' areas of competence, a congregation can make sig-nificant contributions to the well being of the countless individuals whose healing and growth will be influenced by these professionals during their careers.

15. Sprinkle spirituality, caring love, laughter, and a playful spirit generously at appropriate moments through-

out well being programs and in the ongoing life of your organization. The more serious your organization's purposes, the more crucial the light touch can be for its life together. The more conflict that's present, the more need there is for healing and caring communication along with constructive conflict-resolution approaches.

Q. *What are the principles of creative wellness teaching?*

A. Here are teaching approaches that tend to increase people's learning. Joyce Blair Buekers, who sent this summary, has designed and taught well being courses in a variety of church settings, with a more creative style than any other person I know.[4] The experiential approaches she describes reinforce my guidelines mentioned above.

1. Beware of the danger of being only 'in the head' for the whole session. Expose participants to one practical hands-on experience that stresses the theme for the day. It's easy to err on the side of didactic presentations and discussion and have people walk away without enough real understanding to use the ideas they have heard. Each session needs to weave energizing activities that will enliven thoughts as to how to integrate/weave each main concept into the everyday life of participants.

2. The introduction ritual needs to start with an opening question, including the title for the day to help focus on what the group is doing that session.

3. Intentionally engage people in a variety of experiences related to well being. Elicit their passions and experiences about that topic. For example, unearth their

---

[4]Buekers' approach to well being teaching was enriched by feedback from Frank Rogers, professor of education at the Claremont School of Theology in Claremont, California, who has my thanks.

deep connections with the earth, accessing that passion and allowing its energy to hook into the material being presented. On the theme of self-care and earth-care, accomplish this by using symbols, simple rituals, a simple creation song, artistic self-expression, dance, prayer, meditation, or a piece of clay that emerges as a symbol of caring for yourself and/or the earth. Weave these into the presentation of concepts.

4. The concluding exercise should be integrative, pointing to the main theme for the day and how what was talked about is going to impact participants' lives. End with a circle time inviting people to share two things that need strengthening and that they will do between sessions. People need to name what they'll carry forth into their week.

5. The most challenging curriculum is 'How to do it' oriented, but leaders need to present this in their own ways that work for them.

Joyce Buekers highlights her experiences in leading well being groups with this ringing affirmation: "Once well being is embraced by an organization's leaders, it disseminates throughout that organization. One small group meets weekly, then other groups are started from the initial group and there is a definite pyramid effect throughout the congregation or organization. There is no better bonding experience for a church than well being groups."[5]

Q. *Are there relatively simple ways to try a wellness group?*

A. The list of guidelines given above may make the process seem rather complex. There are numerous low-demand ways to try such a program. Of course, as you probably are aware, any new program takes some invest-

---

5. Personal communication from Buekers, July 25, 1995.

ment of energy and commitment. Here are a few ways to begin on an experimental, trial basis:

1. Start small, even if you already sense that a more comprehensive program is needed in your congregation. For example, try a session or two in one class or adult group you sense may be open to discussing wellness issues. Lead the group in one experiential exercise and let them all debrief this in dyads or triads if the group is sizable. If you discover interest in learning more, leave copies with the group's teacher or leader for use by them or other interested persons.

2. Another start-small option is to invite a few interested people to meet informally in your home for an evening to talk about wellness. Overview a few carefully selected highlights of the introductory chapters in one or both texts. Lead one experiential exercise or guided meditation and talk about the spiritual wellness checkups. If people have a meaningful evening, don't be surprised if they spontaneously request to meet again. If those who meet informally are involved in the congregation's life, it may be appropriate to ask what they think about beginning some type of wellness education emphasis.

3. Depending on the responses you get to such a trial run, you may decide to contact a few of the congregation's leaders and teachers to ask if they would be interested in having an introductory, exploratory session on self-other care for a lifestyle of well being. These initial contacts may identify one or more people who would be good candidates to lead a wellness study group, perhaps with a more experienced co-leader like yourself.

Q. *What elements should be included in a well being program?*

A. Each chapter of the two texts—the *Anchoring Your Well Being* participant's workbook and *Well Being*—contains a wealth of exercises and resources. From these and other sources, select a few to highlight in each session. It may help guide your choices of ingredients to know that experience in teaching wellness classes has shown that it is important to spend some time in each session on the following types of materials:

1. Always include some religious disciplines such as scripture, prayer, hymns, or rituals. These help keep sessions spiritually based and anchored in your group's own religious heritage. Each session in the *Well Being* participant's workbook as well as this guide identifies many relevant biblical passages. Include prayers with these. Ask participants to plan and lead these brief periods of spiritual enrichment, celebration, thanksgiving and commitment.[6]

2. Highlight key concepts from the chapters on which sessions focus. This provides easily remembered cognitive maps that are pivotal in each area. The instructor and group members may well rotate in highlighting key concepts, illustrated by concrete examples of how they relate to resolving everyday wellness problems. To illustrate, in discussing the importance of the three basic types of physical exercises, presenters may share their own experiences with each of these or have class members stand and actually try each type briefly.

In presenting the ABCD approach to mobilizing one's coping abilities during crises, presenters can share their own crisis experiences briefly. Inviting others to share their crisis coping experiences encourages group involvement. It is always important to intersperse presentation of ideas with

---

6. Please note that *Well Being* was intentionally written to present a wealth of wellness resources that express the Jewish and Christian understandings of wholeness. But it uses ordinary language without theological or psychological jargon. Although the book is explicitly spiritually centered, its secular language is designed to reach people who ordinarily don't read "religious" books but are hungry for both healthy spirituality and wellness.

opportunities for discussion and experiential exercises. Dividing into dyads of triads for sharing allows everyone to speak without consuming more time than is available, particularly if a group is large.

3. Learning in session will be enlivened if at least one relevant experiential exercise is included, followed by time for some people to tell a little about their experiences. Sessions should often include relevant guided meditations selected from those in *Well Being*. Experiential exercises and meditations help to balance the discussion of key ideas and bring alive in people's here-and-now experience the important concepts highlighted.

4. Each session should include one brief wellness exercise aimed at enlivening people's bodies. Doing physical well being exercises together is another way to balance and quicken the cohesion of wellness groups. This also is a means of learning body well being exercises and keeping the other elements firmly based in body awareness.

5. Near the end of sessions, at-home assignments should be given. These should be related to the topics under consideration and, if possible, to people's developing wellness plans. At the beginning of subsequent sessions, opportunities should be provided for brief reports by participants on what they learned or difficulties they encountered in doing the at-home work. In this way, between-session continuation of wellness learning and practicing is encouraged.

6. Sessions often should include some consideration of how group members can honor their Christian responsibility to help heal the social and environmental roots of individual and family health problems. Evidence is increasing of countless ways in which most if not all health problems have some societal and environmental factors among their causes. People should be encouraged to include the health of their homes, communities, workplaces, and congregations in developing their health-care plans.

Point out that concern for ecological and institutional

justice issues is really enlightened self interest, because helping heal our earth and its institutions can minimize brokenness in everyone's lives. Helping heal the biosphere, the living network of which we are each a small part, is an essential part of holistic well being plans and action.

7. Include some playfulness and humor in each session of classes or groups. The abundant life celebrates all of God's gifts, including gifts of fun, humor, play, and joy.

Q. *In what church settings are well being programs useful?*

A. They can be useful in almost any aspect of a congregation's life. Among the many possible settings are:

• In church school classes for all ages from elementary school through the adult life stages.

• In ongoing groups for youth, women, men, couples, singles, etc.

• In Bible study, prayer, and healing groups.

• In family camps, family clusters, and other transgenerational educational events.

• In teacher enrichment and training groups.

• In worship services and educational lectures.

• In marriage, family, creative singlehood, and parent education programs, especially those for parents of young children who are shaping the wellness attitudes, ethical standards, and behavior of their offspring, for better or worse.

• In neighborhood support and study groups.

• In social witness and community outreach study-action groups.

• In growing-through-crises and grief-healing groups.

• In training sessions for lay caring teams, evangelism, and financial support callers.

• In a congregation's staff retreats.

• In congregational leaders' annual planning retreat.

Q. *What formats for wellness programs have proved effective?*

A. • A sermon series on "Walking the Sevenfold Path of Christian Well Being."

• A brief (45 to 60 minute) mini-introduction to "Christian Approaches to Self-Care for Wellness—for Yourself, Your Family, Your Work, and Your World" to whet people's appetite for self-study or follow-on group sessions.

• A series of weekly sessions (60 to 90 minutes in length), continuing for at least eight weeks. Numerous churches have had such a series offered once each year with good responses.

• A Sunday afternoon and evening well being seminar to introduce participants to the seven dimensions, with the possibility of follow-on evening sessions.

• A weekend well being training workshop aimed at enhancing one's own wellness and also learning to help others do so.

• A Christian wellness Sunday or well being week.

You will find several sample schedules later in this book.

Q. *What type of publicity is most effective?*

A. 1. Choose a name that's descriptive but not threatening to potential participants. Here are some options: "Discovering the Joys of Spiritually Centered Well Being," "How to Enjoy Avoiding Burnout by Better Self-Care," "Self-Care for Women [or Men, Youth, Seniors, Couples, Singles, etc.]"; "Wellness Self-Care for Those Too Busy for Self-Care;" "Loving God by Loving Your Whole Self and God's World."

2. State the group's purposes clearly and positively, including a theological-biblical statement of its objectives.

3. Publicize in your congregation's bulletin or newsletter so that no one will feel excluded, and give personal

invitations to those who seem especially to need the group.

4. Encourage participants in earlier wellness events to give personal invitations to their friends. They are often the most effective recruiters.

5. Develop and publicize well being groups in the context of a congregation's educational ministry. Make it clear that the health education in the group is not a substitute for counseling or therapy.

Q. *What style of leadership maximizes wellness learning?*

A. Leadership that has three characteristics seems to be most effective. These are dialogical interaction, experiential segments, and shared leadership. Dialogical interaction means involving people in vigorous dialogue during the sessions, within the limits of time. Experimental segments means alternating between succinct teaching segments and doing exercises from the texts that will enable the ideas and methods being discussed to come alive in people's experience. These exercises include the checkups and the guided meditations, as well as other experiential components. Shared leadership means involving different group members in one or more leadership functions in each session. This can include things like reading aloud some key paragraphs from the texts, chairing small groups, planning and leading worship experiences or playful segments, or rotating in presiding responsibilities.

Q. *Can the well being approach be used in pastoral care?*

A. Incorporating a wellness orientation can enliven both caring and counseling. Having this holistic perspective in mind can help counselors explore other dimensions of people's lives in addition to the one in which the "presenting problem" is located. For example, it is important to ask depressed clients about their eating, drinking, and exercise pattern. Self-medication of depression by junk food and alcohol, and sedentary neglect of aerobic exercise often increases people's depression. Vigorous exercise is often effective in diminishing depression. In understanding the causes of severe marriage and family conflict, asking about recent loss experiences may illuminate the onset of the relationship chaos. In looking for the roots of many types of physical, mental, and relational problems, it can be useful to look for spiritual and value conflicts that often are deeper contributing causes.

Because most counselees are struggling with issues in one or more of the seven dimensions of their lives, there are many productive ways to use the well being model in counseling. Recommending carefully selected between-sessions reading on their issues frequently increases the productivity of counseling sessions by stimulation of ideas encountered in that reading. For example, reading the chapters on crises and losses in the well being texts can provide insights that help people mobilize their own coping resources.

To illustrate how to use these resources in pastoral care, consider the crucial field of marriage, family, and singlehood education and counseling, including preparation for marriage or remarriage. The chapter on "Nurturing Loving Well Being in Your Intimate Relationships" can be productive homework assignment. In grief education, counseling, and healing groups, the two relevant chapters in the texts offer a wealth of potentially helpful ideas.

The growth orientation of the well being approach also can be a valuable focus in counseling and psychotherapy. Unless these healing arts limit themselves to the old pathology-oriented medical model, they define their ultimate objective as enabling people to move beyond the repair or healing phase to help them learn how to maximize their whole-person wellness. The holistic well being orientation is especially useful in this second phase of the healing-growth process.

Q. *How can wellness in an entire congregation be increased?*

A. Implementing the above guidelines and launching a whole-person, spiritually empowered wellness emphasis in your congregation will probably trigger a process that gradually enlivens your entire congregation. Also, be sure to see the brief section in *Well Being* entitled "Helping Your Organization, Congregation, or Workplace Support Whole-Person Well Being" (pp. 309-314). It points the way to increasing the wellness atmosphere in a variety of religious and secular settings. The congregational wellness checkup included in this book is also a valuable tool.

Q. *Is this a New Age approach?*

A. If a question such as this is asked, it is best to confront such queries head-on by pointing out how the well being approach is a contemporary expression of the Bible's understanding of healing and health. Make it clear that its philosophy *does parallel* certain New Age beliefs, but it finds these beliefs in themes of biblical theology that have been neglected or rejected in much traditional theological thinking. The parallels include a recognition of the wealth of human potentialities; openness to learn from other religions and world views, not just those of the West; and an emphasis on affirming people's strengths and enabling them to develop their God-given inner powers and possibilities more fully.

Having mentioned these parallel emphases, describe the following profound differences between the New Age philosophy and the well being and biblical understanding of people's healing and growth:

1. The biblical and well being views of health understands full, individual wellness as possible only in the context of health-nurturing interpersonal and community

relationships. This is in sharp contrast to much New Age hyper-individualism often called "Me-ism."

2. The biblical and well being views recognize human resistance to wellness-fostering behaviors—sin, brokenness and evil—alongside all the positive potentialities for wholeness in people and society. This realism avoids the superficial optimism in much New Age thinking.

3. The biblical and well being views of healing and health emphasize the dynamic importance of God and our relationship with God. This is in contrast to the vague, amorphous spirituality and the lop-sided over-emphasis on individual human potentialities in much New Age thought.

4. The biblical and well being understanding of God is as the divine Spirit of justice and right, not just of love and peace as in some New Age thought. For Christians, God is most fully revealed in the life and teachings of Jesus the Christ.

Q. *Where can I find additional reading on issues in which there is keen interest?*

A. Good news! Near the end of *Well Being* you'll find the most extensive, carefully annotated list of relevant books of which I am aware. It is organized by chapter topics so you can zero in on those issues that are of particular interest to you and/or group participants.[7] In addition, a variety of relevant resources are available from the Upper Room Spiritual Formation and Healing program.

---

7. See "Recommended Reading to Enhance Your Health and Well Being," pp. 319-335.

Q. *What are some hymns on healing and wholeness?*

A. Here are the titles of relevant hymns:[8]
"For the Healing of the Nations," #428
"Let there Be Peace on Earth," #431
"O God of Every Nation," #435
"Where Cross the Crowded Ways of Life," #427
"Cuando El Pobre (When the Poor Ones)," #434
"Behold a Broken World," #426
"All Creatures of Our God and King," #62
"For the Beauty of the Earth," #92
"Fairest Lord Jesus," #189
"God of the Sparrow, God of the Whale," #122
"Joyful, Joyful, We Adore Thee," #89
"Mountains Are All Aglow," #86
"Dear Lord, for All In Pain," #458
"Heal Us, Emmanuel," #266
"Jesus' Hands Were Kind Hands," #273
"O Christ, the Healer," #265
"When Jesus the Healer Passed Through Galilee," #263
"There's a Balm in Gilead," #375
"We Shall Overcome," #533
"Lord of the Dance," #261
"God of Grace and God of Glory," #577

---

8. Hymn numbers are from *The United Methodist Hymnal* (Nashville, Tenn.: The United Methodist Publishing House, 1989). Many of these are also found in the hymnals of other denominations.

Q. *Is there a well being theme song?*

A. The Hebrew word *shalom* and the Arabic word *salaam* mean spiritually empowered wholeness as well as peace. The song "Shalom," therefore, seems to me to make a fitting musical theme.

Here is an explicitly Christian version: "Shalom to You...Christ be Your Shalom," #666. (The original Hebrew version of "Shalom" is #667.)

Here is a version of this song that I adapted. It lifts up hopes and prayers for *shalom-salaam* in Israel and Palestinian areas and other countries in that troubled part of the world:

> Shalom, my friends. Salaam, my friends.
>> Shalom, Salaam.
> May God's presence here, help us grow in God's love.
>> Shalom, Salaam.
> Shalom, my friends. Salaam, my friends.
>> Shalom, Salaam.
> May God give us *hope*, to make peace in our times.
>> Shalom, Salaam.
> Shalom, my friends. Salaam, my friends.
>> Shalom, Salaam.
> Shalom, my friends. Salaam, my friends.
>> Shalom, Salaam.
> May God give us *strength*, to make peace in our times.
>> Shalom, Salaam.
> May God give us *joy*, to make peace in our times.
>> Shalom, Salaam.
> Shalom, my friends. Salaam, my friends.
>> Shalom, Salaam.
> May God give us *love*, to make peace in our times.
>> Shalom, Salaam.
> Shalom, my friends. Salaam, my friends.
>> Shalom, Salaam.
> May we find well being, to give others the gift.
>> Shalom, Salaam.

I hope you sing with gusto! And add your own stanzas, as I have above.

Q. *How can a congregation's wholeness needs be identified?*

A. Use the following congregational well being checkup to discover the wellness needs of your faith community.

Why and how to use this inventory: The statements in this checkup describe the characteristics and practices of organizations that foster the wellness of their members and constituents. It has two interrelated purposes. First, it can provide a do-it-yourself diagnosis of the impact of your congregation (or other religious organization, or smaller groups within these) on the wellness of people it serves. It does this by identifying the health-enhancing and health-diminishing aspects of its program. Its findings can shed valuable light on the organization's areas of wellness strength and weakness. It thus can provide guidance in developing plans to enable it to become more health-nurturing.

Second, the items in the inventory suggest a wealth of self-care and institutional wellness action-options. These can be used as a checklist from which to select changes needed to increase the wellness educational opportunities within the congregation. Findings from the checkup are as accurate as the collective subjective evaluations of those completing it.

Here are a few of the numerous productive ways to use this instrument in a religious context to fulfill these two basic purposes.

1. The well being task group can use the checkup to provide guidance for designing a congregation's wellness emphasis and events to meet the concrete needs of people within that organization.

2. Professional staff members and lay leaders of a congregation can score the checkup individually and the results then can be summarized. These findings can stimulate

creative planning of particular wellness lifestyle education programs. They also can be used to increase the healthful influence of the congregation's emotional and spiritual climate on all of its people. Using it before an annual re-visioning and program planning retreat can produce many ideas for improving what could be called the overall "wellness quotient" of a congregation.

3. The officers or full membership of the smaller groups within the organization can use the checkup in this same way to evaluate the health of their group and plan wellness programs for their members.

4. A cross section of members can be asked to complete the checkup to provide grassroots feedback for diagnosing and developing a plan to correct a congregation's wellness problems. Such a sample should include some of those who are critical of the current programs.

Congregational/Organizational Well Being Checkup

Instructions: In the following checkup, ignore or rephrase those items that do not apply in their present form to your organization. In front of each statement, place one of three initials:

E = The group is *Excellent* in this matter;

OK = It's *Okay* but there's room for improvement;

NS = The group definitely *Needs Strengthening* in this area.

____ Serious attention is given in the congregation's or organization's program to each of the major dimensions of human well being—physical, intellectual, emotional, relational, work/play, spiritual, ecological, and institutional.

____ There is an emphasis on spiritual healing and wholeness in each of these dimensions of the abundant life.

____ The emotional climate of the organization is characteristically grace-full, accepting and warm, with a strong sense of mutual care, respect, affirmation, integrity, belonging, enjoyment, and shared spirituality.

____ As a result of participating in the organization, people generally feel increased trust, esteem, hope, empowerment, and zest for living. These feelings result from the quality of relationships, the democratic leadership style, and the life-affirming and people-affirming way the group functions.

____ All people within the organization are treated as precious members of one human family, the family of God.

____ People outside the group with radically differing beliefs are also treated with respect as members of God's family.

____ Those who belong for a while usually know each other by name and are interested in each other's well being.

____ People who are absent from meetings know they are missed. If they are absent frequently, someone contacts them to find out if there is a serious problem.

____ The organization's programs address the changing wellness needs and interests of people at different stages of life.

____ Goals within the organization are concrete and measurable, making it possible to know when progress toward them is made.

____ Members understand and generally affirm the organization's purposes, including its wellness objectives.

____ Members have frequent opportunities to strengthen their mental muscles and broaden their intellectual horizons by encountering stimulating people, programs, and/or books from which they can learn.

____ Members are encouraged to learn how to keep their bodies fit by caring for them as temples of the spirit.

____ Members have frequent opportunities in various programs to enrich their spiritual lives and deepen their relationships with God.

____ Lay persons are challenged to discover their own special ministries, using their gifts to reach out to those in need in their church, their community, and in the far-flung parish of the world community.

____ Members learn how to use God's gift of human sexuality in personally and relationally constructive ways.

____ Members have opportunities to grapple with Christian ethical decisions related to the complex personal, family, social, and moral dilemmas in today's society.

____ Members have a variety of opportunities to acquire new insights and skills with which to deepen their important relationships by learning non-violent conflict resolution skills, enhancing spiritual sharing, and nurturing love in these precious relationships.

_____ Parents and teachers have opportunities for training in parenting and teaching for a healthier society (beginning in their own families and communities), focusing on justice issues that block oppressed groups from using their full gifts of God.

_____ Members have opportunities to enhance their caring concern for God's creation by increasing their earth literacy and earth-caring skills, and working together to save the biosphere for future generations of all the children of all the species.

_____ Members have opportunities to learn new ways to cope with crises, losses, and painful transitions. Regular grief healing groups, creative divorce groups, and classes exploring Christian approaches to dying and death are offered.

_____ Members have opportunities to learn ways to avoid burnout and increase their sense of calling in their work and avocational lives.

_____ Members have opportunities to enhance their playfulness and joy as gifts of God to be celebrated regularly together with others.

_____ Members have opportunities to learn how to live with love and zest in their present life stage, by coping constructively with its new problems and developing its new possibilities.

_____ Members are offered encouragement and training in how to work effectively for the overall health of their communities, nation, and world by being peace-with-justice-makers.

_____ Both women and men have opportunities to discover how to cope in healthy ways with the differing wellness needs of each gender in our sexist society.

___ The organization has a high "batting average" in accomplishing its objectives. Tasks usually get done on time, and without undue pressure from leaders on whoever is doing the work.

___ Attendance, financial support, and shared responsibility is generally good, and not dependent on heavy pressure from leaders.

___ Women and men feel equally valued, empowered, at home, and welcomed to participate in the leadership of the organization.

___ If the organization should disappear, those associated with it would feel a strong sense of loss.

___ Both the professionals and the volunteer leaders use a leadership style that is strong, firm, effective, and democratic, enabling the group to accomplish its purposes without excessive conflict.

___ Professional leaders are well trained and competent. They seek to support, coach, and empower the nonprofessional leaders and volunteers.

___ New leaders who are volunteers are selected by a democratic process and rotated regularly so that opportunities to use leadership talents are shared widely.

___ Program planning and implementation are shared widely among the members, enriching this process by fresh ideas and personalities.

___ Decision making on major issues is done democratically, with everyone's viewpoints being heard and respected. Decision making on superficial matters is done by key officers, without taking the time of the wider membership.

___ Leaders demonstrate a strong concern for justice and integrity in their lives and leadership.

___ People feel relatively free to express their ideas, skills, and creativity within the group.

____ Both professional and volunteer leaders usually are sensitive to the needs of members and of other leaders. This includes the need for warm appreciation of their contributions to the organization's life, and the need for their ideas to be respected, especially when these are contrary to the majority view.

____ Sexism, racism, classism, and ageism usually are not present in the structures, rules, customs, or practices of the organization. When these appear, they are identified as problems and corrected expeditiously.

____ People experiencing crises, losses, and painful transitions usually receive caring support from the leaders and members of the organization. It has a care-giving spirit as well as a committee to coordinate reaching out to people in stressful situations. Interpersonal conflicts are handled quickly, fairly, and constructively. When major conflicting viewpoints and agendas are present between sub-groups, creative compromises are negotiated.

____ Problem people, such as those who talk excessively in a monopolizing way, are handled by the leaders compassionately but firmly, so that they are not allowed to interfere with the needs of others or the organization's ability to achieve its objectives.

____ The organization has an effective strategy for discovering and using the latent talents of all its members.

____ Newcomers are welcomed and given encouragement to become full participants in the group by bringing their gifts to its life and work.

____ All members take part in regular evaluations of the organization's programs and policies, and participate in making changes in these. Thus, the communication loop between leaders and members is kept operative.

____ Criticism from members is heard carefully and considered seriously by leaders in planning future events.

____ The group does regular long-range planning to project tentative plans for several years ahead. Input into this planning process from all members is facilitated by regular group self-evaluations and goal setting.

____ Communication within the organization is generally clear, open, honest, caring, and effective.

____ There often is lightheartedness and laughter in the organization, as well as times of serious grappling with difficult issues and conflicts.

____ Members enjoy sharing relaxing recreational times and events regularly.

____ People feel safe enough in the group to risk being vulnerable and honest about their real feelings.

____ When members feel alienated from the group, other members usually take the initiative in reaching out to seek reconciliation.

____ The programs of the organization are designed to meet the basic interests and needs of its present and hoped-for members.

____ Some of the energy within the group is used to reach out to the needs of others outside the group and to increase the well being of the wider community.

____ Belonging to the organization tends to build bridges rather than barriers between its members and other persons and groups with differing philosophies and purposes.

____ There is openness to interact and cooperate with other organizations, rather than being an exclusive or closed group.

____ Commitment to the organization does not involve feelings of superiority over non-members or members of other groups.

____ There is attention to the health of group process as well as the content of the program, to the wholeness of means as well as goals.

_____ There is a healthy balance within the group between left-brain intellectual, rational, and analytic activities, on the one hand, and right-brain intuitive, emotional, artistic, playful activities, on the other.

_____ Members of the organization receive encouragement and opportunities to use their political muscles in a prophetic way to remedy economic and social injustices, and increase the possibilities of all persons to develop their God-given potentialities, throughout their lives.

_____ In spite of its limitations, I'm very glad to be a part of this organization.

How to Use the Findings of This Congregational Checkup

To achieve the maximum wellness benefit for your organization, take these action steps, adapting them to the uniqueness of your situation:

1. Depending on who has completed checkups, summarize the numerical results in terms of the frequency with which each of the three categories were selected. What's an efficient way to do this, if it is not convenient to use a computer? It is to make three columns after each item on a blank checkup form. In one column make a mark for those checking that item as E = The group is Excellent in this matter; in the next column make a mark for those checking that item as OK = It's Okay but there's room for improvement; in the third column make a mark for those checking that item as NS = The group definitely Needs Strengthening in this. Then total the number of checks after each item in each column.

2. On a separate sheet, note any comments and suggestions made by those completing the checkup for your organization.

3. Mark or make a list of items that received a high percentage of E ratings. These are areas of perceived strength and health in the organization. Congratulate the organiza-

tion's leaders and urge them to continue these emphases that clearly are valued by many who completed the checkup.

4. Mark or make a list of items frequently marked OK and NS, as areas that are perceived to need strengthening, in either relatively minor or major ways.

5. Share a summary of the major findings derived from the above four steps with everyone in the organization, perhaps sending the results with a note of thanks to persons who completed the checkup. Point out that these findings will be used to guide both short-range and long-range planning of programs so as to increase opportunities for members to meet their wants and wellness needs as they perceive them, in all dimensions of Christian lifestyles.

Be aware of the pattern of differing needs within the organization, reflected in the fact that many of the same items may have received E, OK, and NS evaluations from different respondents. In planning, select OK and NS items that are judged to be do-able, perhaps starting with those that seem particularly urgent. In each area, decide on what the concrete objectives will be, who will take responsibility for developing a remedial program, when it will be implemented, how movement toward the objectives will be measured and reported to the group.

The well being task group or committee that has responsibility for wellness programs in the organization, is the logical group to coordinate the process of analyzing and utilizing the findings, and then delegating responsibility for addressing the frequently checked OK and NS items.

2. Four Sample Schedules of Well Being Events

Objectives of the First Three Events

It is hoped that all participants will: (1) Acquire increased understanding of the seven dimensions of living holistically empowered by Christian spirituality; (2) learn methods of self-care to nurture healing and wholeness in each of these dimensions; (3) develop an ongoing self-care plan for making wellness a central commitment in their Christian lifestyle; (4) learn to use the two texts on their own as resources for enhancing a well being lifestyle on an ongoing basis.

Each of the first three alternative schedules involves a minimum of ten hours of learning focusing on the eight topics in the session titles of the workbook. The fourth option is a one-session mini-introduction to the challenge of well being as a lifestyle and to the two resource books. This may whet the appetite of participants to learn more about wellness issues.

Schedule A: Local Church Setting

(eight weekly 75-minute sessions or ten 60-minute sessions)

Theme of the series: "Christian Well Being—Making Whole-Person Fitness Your Lifestyle"

Session 1: Understanding the Seven Dimensions of Healing and Wholeness

Session 2: Enriching Your Spiritual Life—Wellspring of Love, Healing, Well Being, and Service

Session 3: Loving and Empowering Your Mind for Healing, Creativity, and Outreach to Those in Need

Session 4: Loving and Empowering Your Body for Fitness and Service in a Needy World

Session 5: Nurturing Loving Well Being in Your Family and Other Close Relationships

Session 6: Increasing Well Being in Your Work and Play

Session 7: Growing through Crises and Griefs; Maximizing Well Being at Each Stage of Your Life's Journey

Session 8: Enhancing Your Well Being by Helping Heal a Wounded World

Schedule B: Local Church or Retreat Setting

(Friday evening and all day Saturday;
eight hour-plus follow-on sessions)

Friday:

5:00 p.m.—Registration, room assignment (if in a retreat setting), book table browsing, healthful beverages such as fruit juices.

6:00 p.m.—Dinner with a healthful menu—e.g., low in fat, sugar, and caffeine; lots of vegetables, grains, and fruit; vegetarian proteins.

6:40 p.m.—Welcoming and getting acquainted, a wellness prayer and hymn, the overall objectives of the event and sharing of individual hopes and expectation.

7:00 to 9:30 p.m.—Workshop sessions 1 and 2 (topics as in the above schedule).

9:30 p.m.—Songfest and devotions on the theme of session 1. Shalom affirmation circle = joining hands in a circle; affirming each other; and singing "Shalom," remembering that this Hebrew word means spiritually energized wholeness.

10:00 p.m.—Healthful evening snacks and fellowship.

10:30 p.m.—Goodnight.

Saturday:

7:00 a.m.—Opportunities for a brisk walk or yoga.

7:30 a.m.—Morning devotions around themes of sessions 2 and 3.

8:00 a.m.—Breakfast with a healthful menu.

8:45 a.m. to 12:15 p.m.—Workshop sessions 3, 4, and 5; two mini-breaks with stretching and breathing exercises and healthful snacks.

12:30 p.m.—Lunch with healthful menu, followed by time for relaxing, walking outdoors, writing ideas for self-care plan.

2:00 p.m.—Workshop sessions 6, 7, and 8, writing self-care plan.

4:30 p.m.—Brief service of celebration and commitment to well being lifestyles, including a Shalom/Salaam affirmation circle. Group evaluation and decision about evening follow-on sessions at monthly intervals if desired.
5:00 p.m.—Departure for home.

Schedule C: Retreat or Local Church Setting
(all day Saturday and Sunday until after lunch or to mid-afternoon)

Saturday:
8:00 a.m.—Registration, room assignment (if in a retreat setting), book table browsing, healthful beverages such as fruit and vegetable juices.
8:15 a.m.—Welcoming and getting acquainted; prayer and hymn on wellness themes; overview of the event's objectives and sharing of individual hopes and expectations.
8:30 a.m.—Workshop sessions 1, 2, and 3 (topics as listed above). Two brief breaks during morning with healthful snacks and body-renewal exercises.
12:30 p.m.—Lunch with a healthful menu—e.g., low in fat, sugar, and caffeine; lots of vegetables, grains, and fruits; vegetarian proteins. Followed by time for relaxing, walking outdoors, writing ideas for self-care plan.
2:00 p.m.—Workshop sessions 4 and 5; one renewal break with healthful snacks.
4:00 p.m.—Free time to play a group game like volleyball, walk outdoors, make notes for self-care plans.
5:30 p.m.—Dinner with healthful menu, followed by hymn sing.
7:15 p.m.—Workshop session 6.
9:00 p.m.—Playshop followed by evening meditations on wellness themes.
10:30 p.m.—Goodnight.

Sunday (if in a retreat setting):

    7:00 a.m.—Opportunities for a brisk walk or yoga.

    7:30 a.m.—Morning devotions on wellness themes.

    8:00 a.m.—Breakfast with healthful nutrition and gentle music in background.

    9:00 a.m.—Workshop session 7 and 8, with time to write self-care plan and to discuss possibility of follow-on sessions if desired.

    11:00 a.m.—Group evaluation. Wellness worship celebration around making commitment to well being lifestyles by self-care plans. Discussion of one or more evening follow-on sessions.

    12:15 p.m.—Light nutritious lunch.

    1:30 p.m.—Shalom affirmation circle.

Schedule D: Local Church or Christian School Setting

(one hour to 75-minute mini-introduction to the seven dimensions of well being)

Opening: Instructor mentions the purpose of the session and tells her or his own wellness story briefly; or shares someone else's story, for example, one of the "Windows of Wholeness" stories in *Well Being.* Shows the texts and passes them around the group.

Overviews the meaning of well being in its seven dimensions and its importance in today's hectic, mega-stressed world. Emphasizes the biblical foundations for living healthy lifestyles as Christians in each of these dimensions.

Leads a brief discussion focusing on group members' experiences and issues related to good health care. If appropriate, asks group if they would be interested in exploring the seven dimensions of healthy Christian lifestyles in greater depth on subsequent occasions.

Closing: A meditation or prayer time asking for God's blessing on efforts to follow in the footsteps of Jesus with his concern for life in all its fullness in all dimensions of people's lives.

3. Example of an Effective Publicity Flyer

You are invited to enroll in a spiritually centered class entitled "Christian Pathways to Self-Care for Well Being."

Purpose: This class will provide a variety of practical ideas and methods for increasing the well being of yourself, your family, your community, and your world. During the class, you will be encouraged to develop a plan to enhance your wellness in each of the seven dimensions of your life—body, mind, spirit, relationships, work, play, and the earth (meaning both the natural and the human environments.) Resources from the Bible and our religious heritage will be presented at each session. This class is part of our congregation's response to the rising concern among our people about issues of health-care and wellness. "Well being" is simply a contemporary way of talking about what the Gospel of John calls "life in all its fullness" (John 10:10) Persons who have taken part in a series like this in other congregations report that they have derived many important benefits.

Time and Place: The class will meet at _____, for one and one-half hours for eight weeks. It will begin on _____ at _____. Participants will be asked to commit themselves to attending regularly and preparing for each session by reading the assigned chapters in the texts.

Leadership: The class will be taught by our pastor and _____, one of our members who is a health professional. A few other resource people may be invited to share their expertise.

Texts: (Copies will be available for purchase at the first session.)

• *Anchoring Your Well Being,* participant's workbook
• *Well Being—Exploring and Enriching the Seven Dimensions of Life.*

Schedule of Topics:

Week 1: Making Christian Well Being Your Lifestyle—Overview of the Seven Dimensions

Week 2: Self-Care to Enrich and Strengthen Your Spiritual Life

Week 3: Self-Care of Your Mind for Healing, Creativity and Outreach to Those in Need

Week 4: Loving and Empowering Your Body for Fitness and Service to a Needy World.

Week 5: Nurturing Loving Well Being in Your Family and Other Important Relationships

Week 6: Increasing Wellness in Your Work and Play

Week 7: Growing through Crises and Losses on Your Life Journey

Week 8: Increasing Your Well Being by Helping Heal a Wounded World.

4. Example of One Person's Wellness Plan

(The first part of this plan consists of items from the checkups and texts that this person decided, after each session, were important for her self-care.)

My self-care goals include caring for my spiritual life:

• By being more aware of everyday miracles in mundane things and people in whom I sense extraordinary spiritual gifts;

• By making my beliefs foster love, hope, trust, self-esteem, joy, responsibility, empowerment, inner freedom, and the acceptance of my body and its pleasures; and help me overcome destructive feelings such as fear, guilt, shame, childish dependency, prejudice, unforgiveness, hate, body rejection, and inner fragmentation.

Caring for my mental life:

• By practicing the fine art of forgiving myself, thus becoming able to forgive others and life;

• By regularly balancing my dominant rational, analytical, verbal, quantitative left-brain activities with intuitive, non-analytical right-brain activities such as music, drawing, gardening, joking, story telling, and imaging.

Caring for my body:

• By enjoying some time each day giving my body self-care to increase its aliveness, its attractiveness (especially to myself), and its power to function with high energy, strength, and effectiveness;

• By sleeping seven or eight hours (or less if my body and mind require less for full renewal), at least four nights each week.

Caring for my close relationships:

• By respecting my partner's differences and accepting the futility of trying to reform him [or her] to be like myself. (A difficult lesson to learn!)

• By avoiding being a people-pleaser and playing phony, manipulative games to be liked or to keep peace at whatever price in my relationships.

Caring for my work life:

• By avoiding overloading my workday with too many demands or unrealistic expectations. When I have many things to do, I'll prioritize and focus on one thing at a time.

• By maintaining constructive relations with most of the people at work and not letting the difficult ones get to me for long. When conflicts arise, I will face them and negotiate fair compromises.

• By not taking my work home with me either literally or emotionally by obsessing over work problems.

Caring for my play life:

• By laughing and playing with others regularly.

• By trying in serious situations to see something at least mildly funny.

Caring for the earth:

• By examining and correcting my lifestyle and the values that guide it, to make these more expressive of my love for both the health of the planet and my own health that I know depends on a healthy environment.

• By practicing both parenting and "friending" for peace, justice, and environmental wholeness.

The insightful woman who developed these self-care plans around the seven dimensions then wisely listed what she called her "specific daily to-do's":

• Find one amazing miracle in the mundane.
• Spend time on one personal hobby—day garden, harp, reading.
• Forgive myself for that day's mistakes.
• Exercise workout—biking, steps, or walking.
• Quit trying to change my husband and instead learn from him.
• Sleep five to eight hours per night; meditate one or two times a day.
• Prioritize, saying "No" when needed, and quit setting unrealistic expectations for myself; focus on one thing at a time.
• Trying to resolve work conflicts immediately.
• Learn not to obsess over my work.
• Laugh more and learn a joke each day.
• Before going to bed, list all outstanding "to do's" and problems, and turn them all over to God.
• Evaluate my lifestyle and direct it toward healthy living.
• Teach and learn about peace, justice, and environmental wholeness from my kids.

5. My Hope and Prayer for You

Let me close on a personal level by sharing my wish and prayer for you the leader. I hope that you will soon make two exciting discoveries. One is that your faith community's effectiveness as a channel to bring God's healing love into the everyday lives of people of all ages can grow dramatically by a well being emphasis group or program. The second exciting discovery is that your own wellness can be enhanced as you develop such a ministry. May God bless you and your congregation with life in all its fullness, as this challenging ministry of healing and health is developing!

If you feel moved to share your experiences or need a response to issues you encounter in this process, drop me a note at:

> Howard Clinebell
> 2990 Kenmore Place
> Santa Barbara, CA 93105, USA
> Fax: 805-682-2816
> E-mail: ClinebellH@aol.com

Well Being Course Evaluation Form

(Before you leave, please take a few minutes to complete this form, evaluating your experience in this group. This will help the leader make our group as valuable as possible for its members. Use the back of this sheet if you need additional room for comments and suggestions. Thank you for your help.)

What hopes and expectations did you bring to the class?

_____

_____

Were these fulfilled and, if so, to what extent?

_____

_____

If not, what changes would have helped fulfill them?

_____

_____

Which aspects of the experience were most useful to you?

_____

_____

What parts were least useful?

_____

_____

How could the instructor make future sessions more valuable for you?

_____

_____

Would you recommend this course to friends? ❏ Yes; ❏ No

What additional topics need to be discussed in classes like this?

_____

Name (optional)

_____

PART II:

GUIDELINES FOR LEADING THE EIGHT SESSIONS

Guidelines for Leading Session 1: Walking the Sevenfold Path of Christian Well Being

Note: Remember that the *Anchoring Your Well Being* participant's workbook contains more material under the heading of each session than can possibly be covered in the time available in many class or workshop periods. It is the leader's responsibility to choose from among the topics, stories, and exercises those that promise to be of the greatest relevance to the needs of participants.

Preparation for the First Session

1. Spend some quiet time in prayer and meditation to prepare yourself spiritually, asking for openness to be a channel through which God's healing, growth-enabling power can flow into the lives of those who come to the opening session. Express your thanks for the opportunity to help yourself and others practice the seven dimensions of well being.

2. Read and reflect on the Preface and Session 1 in the workbook, and also Chapter 1 in *Well Being*, and the Introduction in this leader's guide, deciding which of the activities fit the time that is available and which relate best to the well being needs of those who probably will attend. Mark the exercises, ideas, and stories you may use. Try some of the exercises yourself to get a feel for their dynamics and how you may lead them in the group.

3. Outline a tentative session plan. Include concepts to emphasize, stories and experiential exercises to use, worship segments, and a tentative schedule of topics, noting the time you plan to devote to each. Decide how you will ask those who attend this session to share the leadership of the next sessions. For example, during this session ask for volunteers to take turns leading the brief times of singing and prayer at the beginning or end of future sessions.

4. Decide how you will encourage group members to begin reaching out to others who need healing and self-care.

5. Before the session begins, place chairs in a circle in the meeting room and make certain the temperature is comfortable. Bring flowers or a growing plant. Have equipment to play an audiotape or a CD, and select music to set the tone of a nurturing, lively learning environment. Gather other needed tools such as newsprint and markers that you will need.

6. In all of the workbook sessions, the slash mark (/) means to pause and follow the instruction that has just been given before continuing to the next one. Double asterisks (**) indicate an exercise that can be deleted if your time is limited.

7. Follow these same steps to prepare for future sessions.

Naming Yourself and Your Hopes

Have available some crayons or colored pencils and some three-by-five cards. Ask the participants to take a card and to print on it their favorite name—the one they like to be called by friends. Suggest that they print it large enough that people can read it at a little distance. / Then say to the group, "Think about what you would like to gain in this experience for your well being. It's important that you think of your hopes for this program. By referring back to your hopes later, you can see how much you're able to use this experience for your healing and growth.[9]

Now, below your name, quickly sketch a symbol that expresses these personal hopes. This is not an art class, so don't worry about how it looks. Just relax and let your imagination flow through your fingers."/

Once everyone has finished, take four or five minutes to mill around. Each group member should take both hands of

---

9. It's important to become aware of what your own initial hopes are for this series. By referring back to these, now and again, you can see how much you're able to use this experience for your own growth as a leader.

each person in the group one at a time, and the two should tell each other what their name and symbol means. / With everyone seated again, do a quick "go-round," giving each person a minute or so to say just one or two sentences that express his or her feelings about this exercise. It gives the participants an opportunity not only to focus on their own hopes, but also to connect with other group members. / Suggest to participants that they wear their name card in subsequent sessions so everyone will be able to call each other by name. /

Major Objectives and Themes in This Session

As you lead your group, keep in mind that the following were areas in which opportunities to learn were anticipated in the participant's workbook:

• A foundational understanding of the overall meaning of Christian well being.

• Key definitions and concepts that will be useful throughout this program.

• Two visual symbols and a quick overview of the seven dimensions of well being.

• Tips for using guided meditations, a valuable self-caring method that combines deep relaxation and active imaging to nurture well being.

• Suggestions for starting a self-care plan to fit their particular lifestyle and health needs.

• Some awareness of the challenges and rewards that are available in this study-action program.

To discover the needs and interests of your group, ask participants which of the above topics are of special importance to them. / List these on newsprint identifying these as their learning goals. Point out that it probably will be possible during the limited group session time to deal with their interests only in an introductory way. This can serve to open up topics for further exploration on their own, using the rich resources of the two texts.

Biblical Roots and Resources for Well Being

**Ask group participants to jot in the space provided in the workbook two or three biblical verses or stories that emphasize themes such as healing, wholeness, and the remarkable capacities of humans to develop new strengths throughout their lives. /

Ask for a volunteer to list all the passages on newsprint or a chalkboard. / Invite participants to talk about these and the insights about wholeness and healing they have gained from the stories. Compare and supplement this list with the biblical insights and stories that follow in the workbook. This discussion will strengthen the group's biblical understanding of the nature of Christian lifestyles that foster wellness.

**Awareness Exercise: After the discussion of the biblical passages, introduce this exercise and give the following instructions: "Pause now and reflect on your experiences in our church. When was it most healing and wholeness-nurturing for you? When could it have fulfilled this mission more effectively, in your experience? How could it respond more fully to the present needs of people for healing and growth?" Allow time for people to jot their responses in their workbooks or on paper, then give each person in your group a brief opportunity to share one response to each of these questions.

**Making Visual Motifs of the Seven Dimensions of Well Being

Have a member of your group who enjoys drawing make sizable copies of the two well being images (or make enlarged photocopies of them), so that they can be placed in a prominent place in the room. In this way, everyone in the group can see these images of well being clearly, session by session, as the focus turns to each of the seven dimensions.

A Preview of the Seven Dimensions

The two visual motifs illustrate the holistic approach of seeing the inter-connections among all seven dimensions of our lives. For each of the seven dimensions, ask a member of the group to read the paragraph in the workbook, then encourage group members to discuss each one briefly.

Personal Reflection Exercise: Say to the group, "In light of what you have thought about up to this point, take a few minutes to note in the space in the workbook your personal questions and insights about how the seven dimensions relate to your life as a Christian." / Then enable the group to learn from each other's reflections by doing a go-round, giving each person a brief opportunity to share one or two responses to this question.

What Is a Christian Well Being Lifestyle?

To understand the goal toward which these sessions can help people move, here is an overview of some characteristics of a Christian well being lifestyle. Have members of the group take turns reading each of these characteristics and then have a brief discussion of these as identifying marks of a Christian wellness lifestyle. (If time is limited, just read and discuss the first sentence in each item.)

Hope and Wholeness in a Broken but Birthing World

Participants are asked to jot notes in the workbook about promising, hope-awakening developments they see in the wider world. Ask members of the group to mention, as you list on newsprint, what they see as candles of hope before the dawn.

A Guided Meditation: Experiencing the Seven Dimensions of Well Being

The workbook contains several guided meditations. These exercises will help bring alive the holistic healing and well being ideas you and group participants encounter. Such guided meditation, which combines full-body relaxation and active imaging, is a fruitful way for people to use one of God's good gifts, their imaginations, to enliven their body, mind, and spirit.

This particular guided meditation about the seven dimensions has three interrelated purposes: (1) to provide an opportunity to start learning how to use guided meditations; (2) to enable participants to experience the seven dimensions of healing and well being, on which these sessions focus; (3) to enable participants to enrich their well being, in one or more of these dimensions.

Remind participants that they are always free to stop a meditation if they choose. But encourage them to talk with you later about the meditation if they stop because they feel threatened by something during this exercise.

In future sessions, you can ask a member of the group to read the meditation aloud. During this first session, however, if you read it you can model how to lead such an exercise. Stop at each / for a brief time while everyone, including yourself as the reader, does what is suggested. You may wish to tape record the reading prior to the group session. This frees everyone to participate more fully. Remember that there is no "correct" way to do any guided awareness meditation.

If your group cannot do all seven steps in one session because of limited time, splitting the exercise between two or more sessions is fine. But remember to repeat the preliminary body-relaxation step each time you do more of the steps. This will prepare participants to use the exercise more productively.

Closing Song, Prayer, and Evaluation

To close this session, have a brief period of quiet meditation and prayer, celebrating the learnings, however large or small, that occurred. Give each person an opportunity to share one thing they plan to do for their own wellness between sessions, but do not pressure anyone to speak. Then join hands in an affirmation circle and sing either the song "Shalom-Salaam" or one of the wellness hymns listed.

Take a few minutes to have the group do a brief verbal evaluation of the session's effectiveness as a basis for your planning of future sessions, or if time permits, use the well being evaluation form at the end of Part I of this leader's guide. Ask the participants what they will remember from the session and what needs more clarity. Then remind the group of the between-sessions wellness assignments and mention the theme of the next meeting.

Preparing for the Next Session

1. Complete the between-sessions tasks that group participants are asked to do, both to prepare for the next session and for your own well being. Be sure to take and score the spiritual well being checkup, remembering that the checkups in each session will be used both as a self-evaluation and a self-caring tool. Session by session, model developing your own incremental self-care plan and implement things that seem particularly important to your well being.

2. As you read and reflect on the second session in the workbook, note the things you particularly like and may use in the next session. Try some of the exercises yourself to get a feel for how to lead them in the group. Also read or at least scan Chapter 2 in *Well Being* to enrich your understanding of spiritual wellness.

3. Bearing in mind the feedback from the first session, outline a lesson plan that includes the topics, ideas, stories, and experiential exercises you would like to use, as well as how you will share the leadership with the group's members in the upcoming session. If you didn't line up a volunteer to lead the opening (or closing) singing and prayer times, phone someone and invite him or her to help in this way.

4. Before the group meets, check the meeting room, placing a symbol of spiritual wellness in the center of the

circle. Plan to have some growing plants to enliven the atmosphere and increase the oxygen in the room. Select an audiocassette or compact disk of music that will set the tone for spiritual self-care and learning.

5. Spend some time in meditative prayer, picturing each group member nurtured by the light of your caring and by God's love. Also picture yourself leading the group effectively in ways that challenge and enrich the well being of all persons, including yourself. Thank God for the privilege of leading the group and thus becoming a channel for God's healing love.

6. Decide how you will encourage group members to begin reaching out to each other in self-other caring ways. Remember that wholeness involves self-investment in the healing and wholeness of others. If people invest themselves in encouraging others' search for wellness, their own well being will be strengthened.

Guidelines for Leading Session 2: Enriching and Empowering Your Spiritual Life: The Key to Christian Well Being

Note: If the time in your class or group is limited, delete the sections marked with double asterisks (**).If participants have read Session 2 in their workbooks before the group meets, as recommended, there is no need to read all the sections verbatim.

Major Objectives and Themes in This Session

As you lead your group, keep in mind that the following were areas in which opportunities to learn were anticipated in the participant's workbook:

• Why healthy Christian spirituality is crucially important to all dimensions of well being.

• Fresh ways to enhance spiritual well being and to gain a new understanding of how healthy spirituality is at the heart of a Christian well being lifestyle.

• How to satisfy spiritual hunger in health-enhancing ways and thus become open more fully to the divine Spirit's continuing invitation to well being.

• Resources to enliven spiritual life.

• Spiritual empowerment exercises.

• How to use the spiritual well being checkup to increase religious and ethical health.

• How to strengthen spiritual self-care.

To discover the needs and interests of your group, ask participants which of the above topics are of special importance to them. / It is helpful to list these on newsprint, identifying these as their collective learning goals.

**Sharing Stories: Religious Faith Empowers Healthy Living

Personalize the vital importance of people's spirituality for their overall well being by asking participants to think of individuals they know whose religious faith enables them to live constructive and caring lifestyles in spite of difficulties and griefs. Explain that this individual may be anyone who embodies (or embodied, if they are no longer on this earth) a transforming Christian faith. / Talk together about the religious life of these individuals that enables them to maintain hope, strength, and love despite a situation that may otherwise have produced only bitterness and despair.[10] /

**Encourage several group participants to share briefly some of these stories of spiritually empowered people.

---

10. If people have not known such a spiritually empowered individual personally, read one or two of the inspiring stories in *Well Being*'s windows of wholeness—people whose faith gave them the power to live healthy lives. See the windows of wholeness about Rosa Beyer (p. 5), Hildegard of Bingen (p. 21), George Washington Carver (pp. 55-56), Frank Jones (p. 90), Dorothy Day (p. 155), Harold Wilke (p. 229), and Clem Lucille, my mother (p. 223).

Group Ideas and Planning

Invite the group to look over their checkups, reminding them to keep these issues in mind:
- the NS and OK items checked as important or urgent;
- initial thoughts about steps to take to strengthen spiritual well being.

**To help the participants learn from each other, take a few minutes for people to share what they discovered and plan to do as a result of taking the checkup.

Biblical Roots and Resources

Learning Exercise: Ask the participants to take a few minutes to jot in the space provided in their workbooks a scripture passage or two that emphasize the importance of spirituality in a Christian lifestyle. / Then invite group participants to list these passages on newsprint under the heading "Spiritual Well Being Scripture.

A Spirituality That Hurts or Heals

Follow up the conversation about scriptural passages with the following reflection exercise. Read aloud this statement by Erma Pixley: "Religion can either be a set of wings for our souls to fly or a lead weight around our necks!" Ask the group to think about their own experiences of religion and the church in light of Erma's statement and to consider these questions: "Have you experienced religion that felt like a heavy weight on your spirit? How does your faith provide wings for you?" Invite a few participants to share brief responses with the group.

Seven Spiritual Needs

The seven universal spiritual needs are listed below. Consider the impact of these needs on your own spiritual well being and on your congregation's spiritual health.

1. To experience regularly the healing, empowering love of God.
2. To experience regularly renewing moments of self-transcendence.
3. To develop vital beliefs and a worthy object of devotion that give our lives meaning, purpose, and hope.
4. To develop values, priorities, and life commitments centered in love, integrity, and justice that help us live in ways that are caring and responsible, both personally and socially.
5. To discover and develop the capacities in our souls for wisdom, creativity, and agape love.
6. To experience our deep connections with other people and with God's wonderful creation, the natural world.
7. To develop spiritual resources to enhance our trust, self-esteem, hope, and love of people and life; and to develop spiritual resources to help heal the wounds of grief, guilt, resentment, and self-rejection.

The participant's workbook contains self-care exercises for meeting each of these spiritual needs constructively. Use the contents of that book, plus your own spiritual issues and those of participants, to develop conversation about these spiritual needs as ways to connect with God's life-giving love.

Closing Song, Prayer, and Evaluation

Conclude the session with a brief period of worshipful celebration, led by someone in the group, for the learning that has taken place. Perhaps sing a hymn or African American spiritual expressing highlights of the session. Celebrate the new insight and understanding that has come in this session by saying a brief prayer and perhaps inviting one-sentence prayerful responses from others. You may also sing "Shalom-Salaam" to conclude the session.

Then invite the group to evaluate the session's effectiveness briefly, as a basis for your planning of future sessions.

Ask participants what they will remember from the session and what needs more emphasis. Then remind the group of the between-sessions wellness assignments and mention what will be offered the next meeting.

Preparing for the Next Session

Prepare for the third session in the following ways:

1. Complete the between-sessions tasks that group participants are asked to do, both to prepare for the next session and for your own well being. Be sure to take and score the mental well being checkup. Keep modeling your own incremental self-care plan and implement things that seem particularly important to your own well being.

2. As you read and reflect on the third session in the workbook and Chapter 3 in *Well Being*, note the things you particularly like and may use in the next session. Try some of the exercises yourself to get a feel for their dynamics and how to lead them in the group.

3. Bearing in mind the evaluative feedback from the first two sessions, outline a lesson plan that includes some of the topics, ideas, stories, and experiential exercises you would like to use, as well as those that will respond to needs that have emerged in the group.

4. Before the group meets, check the meeting room and place a candle and an open book as symbols of mental wellness in the center of the circle of chairs. Plan to have some growing plants to green and clean the air and increase the oxygen in the room. Select an audiocassette or compact disc of music that will set the tone for mental self-care and learning. (Inviting group members to volunteer to prepare the meeting room will involve them more and reduce your workload.)

5. Spend some time before the next session in meditative prayer, picturing group members nurtured by the light of your caring and by God's love. Also picture yourself leading the group in ways that challenge and enrich the

well being of all persons, including yourself. Thank God for the privilege of leading the group and ask that you may continue to be a channel for God's healing love.

6. Decide how you will encourage group members to reach out to each other and to people in their daily lives in self-other caring ways. Remember that wholeness involves self-investment in the healing and wholeness of others. If people invest themselves in encouraging others' search for wellness, their own well being will be strengthened.

Guidelines for Leading Session 3: Empowering Your Mind for Healing, Creativity, and Loving Outreach to Others

Note: If the time for this well being class or group is limited, delete sections marked with double asterisks (**). If participants have read Session 3 in their participant's workbook before the group meets, the session can be streamlined by quickly reviewing the main points of each topic without taking time to read them during the session. This will leave more time for discussion and for experiential exercises.

Since many of the participants will have already taken and scored the well being checkup for this session, it is important to provide a brief opportunity, early in the session, for those who did so to share with the group what they discovered about their mental wellness, including any issues that now have heightened interest for them.

Major Objectives and Themes in This Session

Keep in mind what participants will come expecting if they have read this section in the participant's workbook. The session's objectives include:

• The profound interrelationship of mind with spirit and body.

• The roots of mental well being in the Bible.

- How to develop more of the mind's many unused gifts.
- New ways to use the mind for both self-healing and self-caring.
- Methods for increasing creativity, inner joy, and problem-solving ability.
- Ways to use the mind to reach out with informed caring to all persons.
- Strategies for enhancing mental well being.

Again, to discover the needs and interests of your group, ask participants which of the above topics are of special importance to them. / It is helpful to list these on newsprint, identifying these as their learning goals.

Biblical Roots and Resources

**Before highlighting and perhaps discussing some of these passages in the participant's workbook, take a few minutes to ask participants which scriptural passages they thought of when they jotted down some that emphasize the importance of truth-seeking and education for Christians.

What Is Mental Well Being?

Review the criteria for this dimension of wellness, perhaps giving some examples of people who embody what they mean—for example, George Washington Carver as described in the window of wholeness in *Well Being* (pp. 55-56). Then ask participants what they experienced in the learning exercise at the end of this section in their workbook.

Your Mind's Well Being Is Crucial to Your Total Wellness

This session includes important ideas that may be new to some people. Ask participants what they found illuminating or problematic when they read the workbook.

Look over the sections in the workbook that follow—on self-responsibility, exercising your mind, using your mind for stress reduction, resolving destructive feelings, developing your creativity, learning meditation, etc., reaching for help when mental problems hit, and developing a new mind—and decide which ones to highlight. Then decide which of the numerous learning exercises to do during the session. The "Discover Your Hidden Treasure" guided meditation has proved to be particularly effective in my experience.

Stress Reduction

Because so many people in our pressure-cooker society suffer from chronic high stress, focusing on this issue and leading one or two of the stress-reducing exercises will probably be well received in your group.

Questions for Reflection

These can be used to stimulate productive discussion, if there is time in the session.

Adding to Self-Care Plans

Be sure to encourage participants to add a mind-personality wellness dimension to their plans, perhaps giving them some guidance on how to do this. And remind them to continue practicing the parts of their self-care plan from previous sessions.

Closing Song, Prayer, and Evaluation

Close the session by doing three things, either leading them yourself or with the help of a group member.

1. Sing a hymn that expresses the awareness that education is a central task of persons seeking to live a Christian lifestyle. One example is the hymn that begins,

"Open my eyes that I may see, glimpses of truth thou hast for me."[11]

2. Celebrate new understandings by spending a brief time in prayer expressing joy and thanksgiving for such learnings. One way to do this is to join hands in a circle of mutual affirmation and invite people to offer one-sentence prayers, if they wish to do so.

3. Lead a brief oral evaluation of the session, aimed at increasing the benefits to well being of future sessions.

Preparing for the Next Session

Before the fourth session, prepare by doing the following things:

1. Spend some time each day in imaging prayer, picturing group members nurtured by the light of your caring and God's love. Also picture the whole group, including yourself, in its meeting place, being challenged and enriched by learning from you, each other, and the Spirit of truth. Express thanks for the privilege of leading such a group and ask for help in coping constructively with any difficult people in it.

2. Complete the between-sessions tasks that group participants are asked to do. As you take and score the physical well being checkup, continue to develop and start to implement your own incremental self-care plan. Prepare to share a little from your own experiences when you invite others to share theirs. Modeling in this way what you ask group members to do may prove to be the most effective channel for teaching and learning.

3. As you read and reflect on the fourth session in the workbook and Chapter 4 in *Well Being*, note what you probably will use in leading the group. Take time to try the exercises you like. This is the best preparation for leading them in your group.

---

11. Found as number 454 in *The United Methodist Hymnal*, but it also appears in other hymnals.

4. Keeping in mind the evaluative feedback from the third session, outline a lesson plan for the next session. Include topics you will highlight, stories and experiential exercises you will use, how you will encourage group members to implement their self-care plans, and how you will keep incorporating the Christian faith in your presentations. Also decide how you will share the leadership with group members in the upcoming session.

5. Before the session, check the meeting room and place a picture or symbol of physical wellness in the center of the circle. Include some living plants and play some music to improve the atmosphere and ambience in that room.

6. Remember that Christian healing and wholeness involve self-investment in the healing and wholeness of others. Decide how you will encourage group members to reach out to each other, their families, and others in need of healing in the congregation.

7. As you picture group members, one by one, begin to identify the person who seems to have the potential to co-lead future well being groups. In this way, you can gradually help create a leadership pool for a wider program of wellness. Participating in a well-led group is one essential part of training to lead such a group.

Guidelines for Leading Session 4: Loving and Empowering Your Body for Fitness, Pleasure, and Service

Note: If the time available for sessions in your well being group is limited, delete sections marked with double asterisks (**).

Major Objectives and Themes in This Session

As you lead, be aware that participants may come expecting to have opportunities to learn the following:

- Resources for enhancing the loving self-care of the body.
- Biblical guidelines and resources for the body's well being.
- Ways to use the findings of the physical well being checkup.
- Several basic physical wellness exercises.
- How to broaden an overall self-care plan by adding regular exercises for physical well being.
- Some ways to outwit inner resistance and roadblocks to physical health.

Again, to discover the needs and interests of your group, ask participants which of the above topics are of special importance to them. / It is helpful to list these on newsprint, identifying these as their learning goals.

Biblical Dimensions of Physical Health

In the participant's workbook are listed a number of scriptural passages that relate to the body and the way we treat our bodies. I have learned that often people have read these passages many times and have not noticed the obvious connection with the care of our bodies. As you discuss these passages with your group, some may be surprised about these interpretations of scripture.

Useful Experiential Exercises

Consider using several of the following exercises:

1. Lead the group in an awareness exercise in which they seek to experience their bodies as temples of the Spirit.

2. Take the group on a brief walk, leading them in experiencing the difference between a brisk aerobic pace and a leisurely ambling. If part of this time can be spent walking inside and then outside, participants' awareness will be increased regarding the wellness bonuses of being nurtured by nature when they are walking.

3. Lead the group briefly in some of the flexibility

exercises that are described in the workbook's discussion of the body's need for three kinds of exercising. (This is an excellent way to change the pace of a session that has focused mainly on consideration of concepts and discussion of methods. It is also a quick way of enlivening people who may be on the verge of napping.)

4. If snacks and beverages are served before or after the session, make a point of selecting healthful goodies such as fruit and fruit juice rather than the usual high-fat, high-sugar, high-caffeine types.

5. Model your enjoyment of body wellness enhancement and express thanks for the opportunity participants have to discover new strengths, skills, and spiritual aliveness in their bodies. (Preparing and distributing a handout in which you list healthful foods and beverages can help raise nutritional awareness.)

Some Productive Areas for Discussion

The participant's workbook explores a variety of issues that merit vigorous discussion in the session. These include the basic components of body self-care—good nutrition, regular exercise, adequate rest, reducing intake of toxins, and increasing sensual satisfaction. These can be presented as spiritual disciplines for Christians who regard their bodies as temples of the Spirit.

A closely related topic for discussion is what congregations can and should do to become better centers of physical self-care and physical healing, and thus help people integrate their physical and spiritual self-caring. The historical context for such a discussion is the trail-blazing work that Christian congregations and denominations have done in the past and what they are doing today. This includes pioneering in establishing and maintaining hospitals and hospices through the centuries.

The remarkable work of John Wesley, the eighteenth-century Anglican whose work launched the Methodist movement, illustrates this pioneering. In 1747 Wesley wrote

Primitive Remedies: An Easy and Natural Method of Curing Most Diseases. It became the standard home treatment and self-care book for more than a century in both England and America.

Some of Wesley's advice seems remarkably similar to current wisdom about self-care of our health. Wesley was quite aware of the influence of emotions and spirituality on physical health. He wrote, "The love of God . . . by the unspeakable joy and perfect calm serenity and tranquillity it gives the mind, it becomes the most powerful of all the means of health and long life."[12]

Closing Song, Prayer, and Evaluation

Close this session by doing the following things:

1. Sing a hymn, spiritual, or folk song that celebrates the wonders of our bodies or gives thanks to God for the gifts of our bodies.

2. Celebrate new understandings that have dawned in participants' minds during this session by first listing these, and then by expressing gratitude for them in a prayer.

3. Lead a brief evaluation of the strengths and weaknesses of the session, aiming at increasing the wellness benefits of future sessions.

Preparing for the Next Session

Prepare for the fifth session in the following ways:

1. Complete the between-sessions tasks that group members are asked to do. Read Session 5 in the participant's workbook and also Chapter 5 in *Well Being.*

2. As you read this session and take your relationship well being checkup, note which points to highlight in the

---

12. Pp. 19-20. This remarkable book was republished in 1973 by the Woodbridge Press Publishing Co. of Santa Barbara, California.

next session. Also, sketch out your own self-other care plan.

3. Keeping in mind the suggestions and criticisms from the group evaluation, outline a preliminary lesson plan for the next session. Include topics you will emphasize, stories and experiential exercises you will use, how you will share group leadership, and how you will encourage participants to reach out to their families, sharing what they are learning about relationship well being.

4. Decide how you will encourage group members to continue developing and implementing their incremental self-care plans. An effective way to do this is by sharing your own ups and downs and then inviting others to do the same.

Guidelines for Leading Session 5: Nurturing Loving Well Being in Your Intimate Relationships

Major Objectives and Themes in This Session

As you lead your group, keep in mind that participants may come expecting to have opportunities to learn the following:

• Why the quality of close relationships is so important to total well being.

• Biblical resources that can strengthen shared spirituality in intimate relationships.

• Insights about the nature of Christian love.

• Strategies that help resolve conflicts and nurture the growth of love in intimate relationships.

• A valuable do-it-yourself communication tool called the Intentional Relationship Method, designed to help couples or families prevent and heal conflicts, and also cultivate their love intentionally.

• How to strengthen an overall self-care plan by adding steps of caring for others.

Biblical Resources

If group members came up with biblical passages and stories on their own, invite someone to list these on newsprint. / Invite comments and questions about these as well as the passages listed in the participant's workbook. If there is time, an illuminating discussion can center on these biblical teachings.

What Is Christian Well Being in Relationships?

Consider raising issues and inviting feedback concerning the definition of healthy love—"Caring about and commitment to one's own and the other's continuing growth, empowerment, and self-esteem." What does it mean to love ourselves, as in Jesus' instruction to love our neighbor as ourselves? How does one do this in everyday relationships? How does it relate to feeding each other's "heart hungers"—our basic psychological, emotional, and spiritual needs?

Building on Discoveries from the Checkup

Invite participants to share some of the insights gained by taking the checkup—insights about nurturing love in their intimate relationships. And perhaps mention something you discovered using the checkup yourself. Ask about things they have decided to change to enhance their relationships.

The Strategies of Self-Other Caregiving

Having these basic love-nurturing strategies listed on newsprint can help to stimulate recall and discussion in the group. Because there are twelve of them, it is important to ask participants for feedback on the ones that seem particularly important or difficult for them. Also, it is well to ask them what they added as strategy number 13.

The Intentional Relationship Method

Take time to have people experience the first step of this method. If there are couples in the well being group, have them take a few minutes to take turns completing the sentence, "I appreciate in you . . ." With non-couples, simply ask the group to divide into clusters of three and do a brief "go-round" in which they take turns having two people tell the third what they appreciate about her or him. After they have done this, suggest that they debrief the exercise by sharing how they felt receiving and giving the "appreciates."

Beyond Mutual Need-Satisfaction

Focusing on this section provides an opportunity to discuss the nature of self-giving love from a Christian perspective, including how this is health-nurturing in close relationships.

Questions for Reflection

Discussion of these questions can encourage reflection on significant learnings by participants during the session and lead them into "strengthening your self-other care plan" by adding love-nurturing strategies and making changes in their interpersonal behavior with their significant others. It is important to save a little time for them to move ahead in enhancing their plan in this way.

Closing Song, Prayer, and Evaluation

End this session with a brief, lively period of worshipful celebration. Sing a favorite folk song or hymn about God's love and human love. Then join hands and invite people, if they wish, to express prayers of thanksgiving for new insights that may help their relationships flower.

If it was not done at the close of Session 4, have a more in-depth mid-course evaluation, perhaps using the form at the end of Part I of this leader's guide. This will provide you with more extensive critical feedback that can be valuable for doing mid-course corrections as you plan the three remaining sessions.

Preparing for the Next Session

Prepare for the sixth session in the following ways:

1. Do the between-session tasks that group participants are asked to do. Take the work and play well being checkup and spend some time in meditative prayer picturing group members experiencing increasing well being.

2. As you read Session 6 in the participant's workbook, highlight the things that you may use in the next session. Do the same with Chapters 6 and 7 (on work and play wellness) in *Well Being*. This will enhance your resources for leading the sixth session.

3. Remembering the evaluative feedback from group members, outline a tentative lesson plan, including the topics, stories, and learning exercises you would like to include.

4. Decide how you will encourage group members to implement their self-other care plans and also reach out to share well being with others in the congregation.

5. Just before the session, check the room and prepare the things you'll need, including music and several green plants to enliven the atmosphere. Spend a few minutes in that place in meditative prayer, enjoying the presence of the great Teacher of all teachers—God's living Spirit.

Guidelines for Leading Session 6:
Increasing Well Being in Your Work and Play

Major Objectives and Themes in This Session

As you lead your group, keep in mind that the following were areas in which opportunities to learn were anticipated in the participant's workbook:

• Resources for increasing self-care for wellness in both work and play.

• Insights from the Bible to illuminate these two key areas of living.

• How to use the checkup to evaluate the strengths and weaknesses of work and play self-care.

• Strategies for avoiding burnout in your work and for implementing your Christian mission in both your vocation and avocation.

• Playful self-care strategies to enliven and energize your lifestyle.

• Suggestions for encouraging family members to increase their general wellness by balancing work and play.

• Suggestions for encouraging leaders of your congregation to integrate more healthy work and play in their education and programs.

To discover the needs and interests of your group, ask participants which of the above topics are of special importance to them. / It is helpful to list these on newsprint, identifying these as their learning goals. Then point out that it will be possible during the limited group session time to deal with their interests only in an introductory way designed to highlight key insights. This can serve to open up topics for their further exploration on their own, using the rich resources of the two texts.

Point out to the group that this session deals with two interrelated topics, both of which are crucial to people's overall wellness—work and play. If you discover that several participants have a particularly strong interest in one or the other of the two topics, it would be well to ask the group to consider scheduling an extra session to deal with laughter and playfulness, so that this entire session can focus on burnout and well being in the workplace.

Since many of the participants will have already taken and scored the well being checkup for the topic of this session, it is important to provide a brief opportunity, early in the session, for those who did so to say something about what they discovered about their work and play wellness.

Biblical Roots and Resources

**If there is time, a lively discussion of scriptural foundations for Christian understanding of work wellness and play wellness can be meaningful for participants. It is especially worthwhile to discuss humor, laughter, and playfulness in a biblical and Christian context, since participants may have never thought about these as essential ingredients in *healthy* religion. This discussion can lead to your highlighting of the reasons why enhancing wellness in both our work and play is so important to healthy Christian lifestyles.

Work Well Being

Have the group talk for a little while in groups of two or three about how they really feel about their work. Ask them such questions as the following:

• Is your work a source of self-esteem and satisfaction that nurtures your well being, or the opposite?

• Do you find anything like the work-generated spiritual meaning and joy described in the workbook?

• If you were not paid for your work (or if you are not paid because you are retired), are parts of your job satisfying enough that you would do it "for free" as a volunteer?

• If well being in our workplaces is crucial to living life in all its fullness, what is a Christian response to individual and societal work crises?

After people have discussed these questions in small groups, gather the whole group together again. Ask them to share any general insights they gained in the discussion.

As an important part of the discussion of well being in the workplace, focus on resources for avoiding burnout, a widespread problem in today's high-pressure society. There are several sections in the participant's workbook and a more extensive section in Chapter 6 of *Well Being* that offer many ideas and methods related to this topic. The use of spiritual resources for preventing burnout should be highlighted.

In discussing Christian attitudes toward recreation and play, emphasize the fact that this aspect of many people's lives tends to diminish rather than enhance their overall health and well being. Focusing on the characteristics of health-giving recreation can be a salutary consideration for those addicted to the many destructive forms of recreation that are anything but re-creating for them. The medically documented healing power of laughter and playfulness can be discussed in this context.

Playfulness and Laughter Exercise

Invite group participants to have a brief, playful joke-telling contest. Ask the group to agree to avoid jokes that put down any group except their own, including jokes that are sexist put-downs. (An alternative to such an agreement is simply to make sure that in the discussion after this contest, people are encouraged to be aware of how different jokes carry problematic messages for certain groups.)

Begin by offering each person who wishes to do so a chance to tell the funniest joke they remember. (Those who can't remember jokes can be valuable participants by groaning or laughing loudly at other people's jokes.) / Second, "tell the most stupid joke you have heard." / Now, the worst pun. / Now, the funniest religious joke. / If there is time, invite the group to use their imagination to come up with other types of jokes. / If possible, have a playful vote after each category for the best and worst jokes of that type. / Enjoy!

A Guided Meditation

There is a variety of effective exercises in the participant's workbook, one or two of which should be chosen to intersperse with and balance the discussion of ideas and methods of self-care. The "Guided Meditation to Enhance Work-Play Well Being," using our imagination to experience boxed-in-ness and playful freedom, is an effective experience for most people.

Select one person to read aloud the instructions for this
guided meditation, pausing at each (/) to participate in the
meditation. You can participate along with the rest of the
group. Following the exercise you could invite people to
share their experiences with one another.

Enhancing Your Church's Programs for Work and Play Well Being

This challenging area of concern for wellness-focusing congregations merits at least brief attention during the session.
Out of this discussion may emerge decisions to help
influence church programming around work-and-play
issues.

Questions for Reflection

These can stimulate further reflection and decision making
on the part of participants regarding what they will do to
enhance their wellness in these twin areas.

Closing Song, Prayer, and Evaluation

Close the session with the following activities:

1. Sing a hymn, spiritual, or folk song that celebrates
the good gifts of God, including satisfying work and joyful
play.

2. Celebrate in prayer any useful insights and new plans
that people have made during this session. Invite one-
sentence prayers of thanks for this growth and prayers of
commitment to implementing individual self-care plans.

3. Lead a brief evaluation of the strengths and weaknesses of the session, aiming at increasing the benefits of the
last two sessions.

Preparing for the Next Session

Prepare for Session 7 in the following ways:

1. Spend at least a brief time each day in intercessory

prayer, imaging each member of your group, including yourself, surrounded by the growth-enabling energy of God's love and your caring.

2. Complete the between-sessions tasks that group members are asked to do.

3. As you read the session in the workbook, take the crises and losses well being checkup and read Chapters 9 and 12 in *Well Being*. List the things that you may want to include in Session 7.

4. Keeping in mind the feedback from the group's evaluation in the last session, outline a preliminary lesson plan for Session 7. Include topics you will emphasize, stories and experiential exercises you will use, how you will share group leadership, and how you will encourage participants to reach out to others, sharing what they are learning with family members and perhaps in the congregation.

5. Decide how you will encourage group members to continue developing and implementing their incremental self-care plans. An effective way to do this is by sharing your own ups and downs and then inviting others to do the same, if they wish.

6. Remember that empowering people by helping them learn how to grow psychologically and spiritually in their crises and losses is a privilege.

Guidelines for Leading Session 7: Growing Through the Crises and Losses on Your Life Journey

This session turns in a different direction than the previous sessions. They focused on growth in dimensions of our lives. In contrast, this session deals with the painful side of life—the crises, losses, disabilities, disappointments, and painful transitions that hit all of us sooner or later. Doing all we can to prepare ourselves for these and learning to cope constructively when they come is an essential part of maintaining well being throughout our lives.

Leading this session may offer more challenges than the others, but it also offers opportunities to help participants enhance their ability to cope with the rude intrusion of crises and losses in ways that enable them not only to cope but also to grow a bit psychologically, spiritually, and interpersonally.

Major Objectives and Themes in This Session

Keep in mind the following areas in which opportunities to learn were offered in the participant's workbook:

- Resources for handling crises and losses.
- Wisdom from the Bible on dealing with crises and grief.
- Awareness and appreciation of all that you already have learned about coping with crises.
- Strategies for helping yourself and others when you or they are going through deep water.
- Ways to strengthen a self-other care plan by adding care before, during, and after times of stress.
- How to help a congregation develop innovative educational and caring group programs to help people find growth and healing in crises and losses.

To discover the needs and interests of your group, ask participants which of the above topics are of special interest to them. / It is helpful to list these on newsprint, identifying these as their learning goals.

Debriefing the Checkup Experience

Since some of the participants will have already taken and scored the crisis and losses well being checkup, provide a debriefing opportunity.

Biblical Roots and Resources

Starting with an overview of biblical passages which participants recall as well as those in the workbook, initiate a discussion of scriptural insights concerning coping constructively with life crises and losses. This discussion can provide an opportunity for you as well as group members to share some experiences of finding resources for handling griefs constructively.

Be aware that many people in congregations are among the "walking wounded." These are people who are functioning adequately, at least on the surface of their lives, but at a deeper level they are paying the price of ongoing infected grief wounds that have not healed, even though they may relate to losses sustained many years ago. Discussing the topic of this session may cause them to become aware of these wounds again. You may discover that the session has become a kind of grief group.

If so, remember this can be a constructive development in that it can point individuals to healing "grief work" which they may need a pastoral counselor's help in doing. Don't be surprised if, after a moving and meaningful session, the group asks to spend another session on these issues.

Learning Exercises

You will find several effective exercises in the participant's workbook that can be used in the session to balance the discussion of ideas and methods of self-care. The one at the end of "Two Biblical Perspectives" can be a productive one to include. A powerful learning exercise that can enable some participants to experience the central theme of the session—how to grow through losses—is the one entitled "Experiencing Healing in a Crisis or Loss." If you choose to use this one, several suggestions are in order.

First, it can put people in touch with unhealed grief, as described above. Second, after you lead it, be sure to have

people talk in pairs, sharing whatever they wish about what
they experienced and learned. While this is taking place, be
alert for anyone who may be crying or otherwise indicating
that they are in touch with painful grief. Then have
everyone debrief in the whole group. If you sense that a
one-on-one conversation with someone is in order, you can
do this after the session, perhaps recommending that they
could benefit from some sessions with a competent, caring
counselor.

Here is another exercise that teaches helping skills. Ask
the group to think of questions and statements that they
believe will encourage grieving people to continue
expressing their memories and feelings. Have a member of
the group list these statements on a chalkboard or piece of
newsprint. (If the group has difficulty thinking of questions,
suggest these: "What happened?" "What are your real
feelings about what has happened?" "How are you doing,
really?" /

Then have the group break into pairs in which they can
take turns practicing responsive, focused listening, using the
questions and statements they formulated. One person
should play the role of a bereaved person, perhaps by
relating a personal experience of loss. The other person
listens intensely and responds so as to draw out any other
painful feelings. Warn the listeners to resist trying to make
the person feel better or solve his or her problem quickly.
Neither of these is possible in the early stages of loss. /

After ten minutes or so, stop the exercise and encourage
each person to evaluate candidly what was and was not
helpful. / Then ask them to reverse roles and repeat the
practice. / Caring listening is a valuable skill to know and
can help people respond more sensitively to a grieving
person.

The ABCD Method

If you understand and have some crisis counseling skills, you can role-play the steps of this crisis helping approach, stopping to point out to the group when you move from one step to another. For example, you can demonstrate responsive, focused listening with warm caring which is the primary way of achieving or strengthening a healing relationship by someone in crisis (the A step).

If some members of the group express interest in being trained in crisis helping skills, they may be candidates for your congregation's lay caregiving team to support individuals and families in painful life transitions and losses.

Enhancing Your Church's Grief and Crisis Program

This session may create an increased awareness of the need for making crisis-coping education, grief healing groups, and training for lay caregivers available more widely and regularly in the life of your congregation. Nothing that a church can do has greater potential for contributing to healing and well being than taking necessary steps to create such opportunities. It may be that some of the group participants will serve on a crisis and grief task force to create such a program.

Questions for Reflection

These can stimulate further reflection and decision making on the part of participants regarding what they will do to enhance their wellness in dealing with crises and grief constructively, and perhaps even growing spiritually as an unexpected asset derived from this pain.

Closing Song, Prayer, and Evaluation

Invite group participants to close this session by doing the following things:

1. Sing a hymn, spiritual, or folk song that celebrates the fresh insights that dawned in this session about caring for one another in crises and losses. Natalie Sleeth's "Hymn of Promise" offers a powerful witness to God's love in the midst of crisis. She wrote this hymn while her husband was dying of cancer, and it expresses a tremendous affirmation of God's renewing grace.

2. Highlight and celebrate the new plans that people have made during this session. Invite prayers of thanks and commitment to implementing them.

3. Lead the group in a brief evaluation of the strengths and weaknesses of the session, aiming at increasing the wellness benefits of the next and final session.

4. Make plans for the final session, including a closing celebration and commitment to ongoing wellness self-care.

Preparing for the Next Session

Prepare for leading the eighth session by doing the following:

1. Complete the between-sessions tasks that group members are asked to do.

2. Read Session 8 and take the ecology-justice-peace well being checkup. Highlight and make notes about things to emphasize. To enrich your knowledge for teaching the last session, be sure also to read Chapter 8 in *Well Being*.

3. Begin sketching out your own self-and-earth care plan so you can speak from your experience as you encourage others to create their plan.

4. Keeping in mind the feedback from the evaluation of the last session, outline a preliminary lesson plan for Session 8. Include topics you will emphasize, stories and experiential exercises you will use, how you will share group leadership, and how you will encourage participants to reach out to others, sharing what they are learning.

5. Decide how you will encourage group members to continue developing and implementing their self-care plans.

6. The next session is the last in the series, unless you and the group decide to continue meeting. Decide how you will help participants deal with any grief or other feelings about the end of the series, and continue their self-care on an ongoing basis. (Ending a meaningful group may awaken grief feelings that can give an entree to other grief experiences that still need healing.) Be aware of your own feelings about the approaching terminus and decide what you will do if the group wants to continue.

7. Most important of all—enjoy! Helping people discover new strength, skills, and spiritual aliveness in their whole being can be fun as well as a privilege!

Guidelines for Leading Session 8: Helping Heal God's Wounded World

This session turns us in yet another crucial direction. It deals with the brokenness, violence, and ill health of our social and natural environments. Its central idea is that these social and ecological pathologies impact and diminish our wellness constantly, and for this reason, helping to heal these is an essential contribution to our own health.

Experiencing the Ecological Circle

Before the session, ask someone to prepare a large drawing of the ecological circle to use as a visual image for stimulating discussion. Invite them to mention ways they experience God in nature. If possible, use the self-teaching exercise in the participant's workbook by inviting participants to take a minivacation from being inside the class, and take a walk outdoors, seeking to experience the three dimensions of the circle.

Major Objectives and Themes in This Session

As you lead your group, keep in mind that the following were areas in which opportunities to learn were offered in the participant's workbook:

• Why seeking individual and family well being, while ignoring the well being of society and the earth, is not an effective way to enhance their overall wellness.

• Why working to heal society and the earth is essential to an enlightened and relevant Christian lifestyle in today's turbulent, deeply troubled society.

• The spiritual and ethical causes which are at the roots of the global ecology-justice crisis.

• Special roles of women and men in saving a healthy earth for future generations.

• Resources in the Bible that provide a foundation for earth-caring and justice-making expressions of Christian faith.

• The unique and essential contribution that all religious people, including Christians, can make to transforming society and saving a viable planet.

• How to understand and use the three dimensions of the "ecological circle" as a model for earth-caring and justice-making.

• Insights and methods for healing ourselves by healing the earth and society.

• Methods to motivate Christians in a faith community to become involved in earth-caring, peacemaking, and justice-creating work.

• Practical strategies by which Christians and congregations can make a positive difference in their world.

• Two earth-awareness guided imaging tools.

• Suggestions for strengthening self-other care plans by adding earth-caring, and suggestions for continuing to use overall self-care plans in the future.

To discover the needs and interests of your group, ask participants which of the above topics are of special importance to them. / It is helpful to list these on newsprint as their learning goals.

Using the Checkup Experience

Some of the participants will have already taken and scored the checkup to prepare for this session. It is important to provide a debriefing opportunity, early in the session, for those who did so.

Biblical Passages

List the ones chosen by participants on newsprint and compare them with the list of justice, peace, and earth-care scripture passages in the workbook.

Choosing Experiential Learning Exercises

This session is packed with possibilities. Consider using several of these enlivening, discussion-sparking exercises:

The exercise at the end of "A Biblical Perspective" in which participants are asked to put themselves inside Jesus' experience in his hometown synagogue.

Ask participants to recall and then share personal experiences that awakened hope for God's world—like the story about the Palos Verdes Blue Butterfly.

The guided meditation, "Discovering What Nature Gave You in Your Childhood," is a valuable way to help people experience a central point of the session by becoming aware of their rootedness in the natural world.

An imaging exercise that can raise people's energy level and motivation for helping insure that future generations inherit a healthy and healthful environment is the one in which they are asked to picture their children, grand-children, nieces, or nephews.

The "Self-Confrontation Awareness Exercise" helps people to examine the earth-friendliness of their lifestyles, and to take steps to express their respect and love for God's creation by their day-by-day living.

"Women's and Men's Special Role in Earth-Caring" can stimulate a spirited dialogue among participants of the two genders about how they understand their special opportunities. The story of Wangari Mathai is a source of hope and encouragement for many people who suffer from social-concerns apathy or burnout.

If your group is meeting after dark on a clear, moonless night, go outside and let them experience "An Exercise to Renew Your Sense of Wonder."

"An Earth-Loving Wellness Exercise" is a powerful way to increase people's awareness of what is at stake in the global eco-justice crisis. It also has the effect of motivating some people to become more active in earth-caring, justice-increasing, and peacemaking actions.

Using "Christian Strategies to Help Save God's Earth"

This checklist is an effective way to enable participants to get more involved in environmental, justice, and peacemaking work as an expression of their faith.

Questions for Reflection

These can stimulate further reflection and decision making on the part of participants regarding what they have decided to do to enhance their wellness and that of the world around them.

Assisting with Self-Other-Earth Care Plans

Some people will need and appreciate your help in completing their overall plans and your guidance about their moving ahead to implement them. It's well to point out that doing the things they have decided will enhance the seven dimensions of their well being and can be a continuing reward of having invested their time and attention in the class.

Reaching Out

If the series has gone well, the group may be excited by the idea of working together on a project aimed at encouraging others in the congregation and the wider community to become involved in wellness-enhancing study and actions. And if this final session has produced increased commitment by participants to helping to heal God's wounded world, they may decide to lead an ecological and justice project that will help the congregation and its wider community adopt more sustainable, earth-saving practices.

Closing Song, Prayer, and Evaluation

Close this session and the series by singing a favorite nature hymn such as "For the Beauty of the Earth" or "Fairest Lord Jesus." Then ask the group to join hands in an affirmation circle as you lead them in this informal ritual, by saying: "A well-loved verse from John's Gospel begins with the words, 'God so loved the world.' Remembering that God loves the whole world, including all people and all of creation, I invite you to complete three sentences that I will begin, with one, two, or three words that come to your mind." Then read each sentence in turn, giving participants the opportunity to complete them with their own words. At the end of the exercise, conclude with a hearty "Amen."

> God so loved the world that I feel . . .
> God so loved the world that I have hope
> and pray for . . .
> God so loved the world that I will seek to . . .
> Amen.[13]

Follow this ritual by inviting group members to offer one-sentence prayers of thanksgiving, if they feel moved to express their feelings in this way.

---

13. I am indebted to Gary Gunderson of the Interfaith Health Program of the Carter Center for this exercise.

Have written evaluations of the entire series, followed by oral evaluative sharing by group members. This dual process provides opportunities for everyone to participate in the evaluation and to make suggestions about how the next well being group could be made more helpful. This evaluation also provides a time for the group to express their appreciation to the leader and plan a reunion, if the group decides to have one.

Periodic reunions have proved to be useful in encouraging people to continue using their self-other-earth care plans and to modify them to make them more effective. You may mention future health-care programs that the congregation plans to offer. Ask for group members' suggestions concerning issues that would meet wellness needs, ways to encourage other people to participate, and who will volunteer to help in needed programs.

Well being groups and classes often enjoy closing a series with a party (featuring healthful refreshments) to affirm and celebrate the friendships and growth that participants have experienced.

Health and shalom, my friends!